DÉLICES CRÉOLES

CAKES

Délices Créoles

Cakes

Exotic Desserts from the French Caribbean

KÖNEMANN

Acknowledgments

Level of difficulty of the recipes:

✩   easy
✩✩   advanced
✩✩✩   challenging

Original edition 1997 © Fabien Bellahsen und Daniel Rouche
Photos: Studio Lucien Loeb/Didier Bizos
Original title: Délices des Îles - Tartes, Tourtes et Gâteaux

Recipe Coordinator:
Jean Bordier
Meilleur ouvrier de France, Président d'Honneur de l'Association des Maîtres Cuisiniers de France, Membre titulaire de l'Académie Culinaire de France, Chevalier de l'Ordre National du Mérite, Officier du Mérite agricole

Chefs, Pastry Chefs and Confectioners:
Michel Comby
Maître Cuisinier de France, Membre titulaire de l'Académie Culinaire de France, Officier du Mérite agricole, Vainqueur du 1er Trophée Taittinger
Honoré Confiac
Diplome d'Argent et Médaille d'argent de la Société de Pâtissiers Français, Responsable du Département Boulangerie-Pâtisserie, "Pâtisserie-Conseil"/Guadeloupe
Joël Kichenin
Professeur technique des métiers de bouche, Membre du Groupement Proessionnel des Métiers de l'Hôtellerie et de la Restauration/ Guadeloupe, Finaliste de la Coupe de France de Pâtisserie 1997, Vainqueur du Trophée du Mérite international 1997
Alain Nonnet
Maître Cuisinier de France, Membre titulaire de l'Académie Culinaire de France, Chevalier de l'Ordre National du Mérite, Officier du Mérite agricole
Frank Saksik: Chef-Pâtissier
Olivier Garrivet: Assistant-Pâtissier

Copyright © 1999 for the English edition
Könemann Verlagsgesellschaft mbH
Bonner Straße 126, D-50968 Cologne

Translation from French: Clémence Scouten
English-language editor: Enid Karr
Coordination and typesetting: Agents - Producers - Editors, Overath
Reproduction: Reproservice Werner Pees, Essen
Production manager: Detlev Schaper
Printing and binding: Leefung Asco Printers Ltd., Hong Kong

Printed in China

ISBN 3-8290-2763-X

10 9 8 7 6 5 4 3 2 1

Contents

Foreword

The arts of cooking, baking, and confection-making have always played an integral role in festive occasions the world over, and are an especially important part of French cultural heritage. In recent years the interest in less familiar regions and their culinary traditions has grown. The series *Délices Créole: Exotic Desserts from the French Caribbean* is dedicated to the sweet delicacies of that distant island paradise. The three volumes—Desserts, Cakes, and Confections— reveal a wide array of new and exotic recipes.

Renowned chefs, pastry chefs and confectioners from France and the French territories in the Antilles invite you to discover the delicious possibilities offered by the wide variety of island produce available today. They would like you to explore their culinary world, in which luscious fresh fruits and fragrant spices form the basis of recipes as surprising aas they are succulent. Readily available tropical fruits such as kiwi, pineapples, oranges and melons, as well as lesser-known types such as mangos, carambolas (or star fruits), kumquats and guavas, are used in most of the recipes. These experts have created subtle, daring and sometimes unexpected combinations which are sure to inspire your imagination and teach you something new about the possibilities of marrying taste, color, flavor and fragrance.

Even local products take on a surprisingly exotic flavor when combined with ingredients like curry and cardamom, ginger and aniseed, coconut and rum. From simple sweets to refined delicacies that will delight even the most finicky gourmet, these recipes conjure up images of warm sunshine, sandy beaches, and palm trees.

This collection of recipes takes you on a culinary journey to an exotic island paradise full of vibrant colors, aromas, and fragrances. The detailed step-by-step instructions and color photographs make it easy for you to try the recipes on your own. Suggestions for substitutions and variations in flavors are provided along with the recipes, so your efforts are sure to be successful. In addition, each recipe is accompanied by an informative text describing the culture and tradition of the region or the historical background of a recipe and the origin of its ingredients.

The chefs hope that they have been able to convey their love of their craft in the volumes of this series. Allow yourself to be carried away to the sensuous pleasures of the islands, and spoil your family and guests with some of the finest delicacies paradise has to offer.

Bon appétit!

Tropical

For the egg-white pastry:
(see basic recipe)
3 egg whites
5 tbsp/75 g butter
¼ cup/60 g sugar
2 cups/250 g flour
a pinch of salt
¾ cup plus 1 tbsp/75 g grated coconut

For the filling:
1 lb/500 g passion fruit
scant 2½ cups/600 ml milk
1 envelope granulated gelatin
a pinch of *poudre de colombo*
5 egg yolks
½ cup plus 2 tbsp/150 sugar
6½ oz/100 ml heavy cream

Serves	*6*
Preparation time:	*1 hour*
Cooking time:	*30 minutes*
Chilling time:	*1 hour*
Difficulty:	★ ★

With its romantic shape and evocative name, one easily imagines this pie as the perfect Valentine's Day dessert. Coincidentally our chef hails from the town of St. Valentine in the heart of Berry, France.

The *poudre de colombo* used in this recipe is a traditional blend of spices including coriander, mustard, nutmeg, garlic and chili peppers. It livens up many Caribbean recipes. The combination of the *poudre de colombo* and passion fruit gives this pie its distinctive and exotic flavor. However, one must use the *poudre de colombo* with restraint to avoid overpowering the flavor of the other ingredients.

For best results, our chef recommends the cream used for the filling should be very cold. It is necessary to blend the whipped cream into the flour mixture rapidly, so as not to allow the gelatin to harden and prevent the flour from mixing in properly.

The lemon juice traditionally used in this type of egg-white based dough has been omitted, as the passion fruit has enough flavor to carry the pie alone. Powdered almonds, suggested in the basic recipe at the end of this volume, may be substituted for the coconut in the pastry.

The combination of different flavors in this pie is sure to stir the passions of your guests.

1. Prepare the pastry following the basic recipe, but substituting the ingredients listed above. Fold the beaten egg whites gently into the dough. Let rest 30 minutes, then roll it out. Fit the crust carefully into a heart shaped pan and prick it with a fork. Prebake twice, for 15 minutes each time, at 390 °F/200 °C.

2. Slice the passion fruit in half and scoop the pulp into a bowl. Stir in the milk. Strain the mixture, saving the liquid. In a separate bowl, combine the gelatin first with a little cold water, then a little warm water. Stir it into the liquid, then add the poudre de colombe.

Passion Pie

3. Beat the egg yolks with the sugar. Quickly stir in the passion fruit before the mixture hardens.

4. Whip the cream and fold it into the batter. Fill the pie crust halfway. and refrigerate for 30 minutes. Pour in the remaining batter and refrigerate an additional 30 minutes. Decorate with passion fruit seeds. Serve cool.

Brioche and

1 kiwi
2–4 strawberries
½ papaya
3 litchis
1 small mango
1 guava
1 pear

For the brioche:
2 tbsp milk
4 cups/500 g flour
2 tbsp/30 g sugar
1½ cup/ 375 g butter
4 eggs
1 tbsp/15 g salt
1 oz/30 g compressed fresh yeast*

For the pastry cream: (see basic recipe)
1 cup/250 ml milk
2 egg yolks
3½ tbsp/50 g sugar
4 tsp/10 g flour
2 tsp/5 g cornstarch
1 vanilla bean
3½ tbsp/50 ml dark rum
½ cup/80 g raisins

For the garnish:
a few fresh mint leaves

Serves	*8*
Preparation time:	*2 hours*
Cooking time:	*35 minutes*
Resting time:	*30 minutes*
Difficulty:	★ ★

Here is a truly wonderful opportunity to use up the fruit lying around your kitchen instead of letting it spoil. The only difficulty in this recipe lies in the proper cutting of the brioche. With just a dash of dexterity and a careful hand, however, the brioche will look beautiful.

The fruits listed in the ingredients are our chef's suggestions, but feel free to use any fruit you have on hand if unexpected guests turn up. This dessert is a welcome alternative to the traditional fruit salad. Small, individual brioches can be used as well. They will make a very eye-catching and easy-to-serve dessert. The fruit should be diced into what the French call a *mirepoix*. To prevent the brioche from absorbing the fruit juices and becoming soggy and unappetizing, the fruit should

only be added at the last minute. On the other hand, the pastry cream will not affect the consistency of the brioche and can be spread in advance.

A bowl of rum raisin or vanilla ice cream, or perhaps a custard, will make a delightful accompaniment to the Brioche and Fruit Medley.

By following these suggestions you should avoid any complications. This beautiful dessert is sure to please both adults and children.

*In hot climates and tropical regions, active dry yeast should be substituted for the compressed fresh yeast, halving the amount.

1. Dice the fruit evenly. Prepare the brioche following the directions in the basic recipe but substituting the ingredients listed above. Place the dough in a buttered brioche mold. Cover with a dish towel and let rise about 30 minutes (depending on room temperature). Bake for 30 minutes at 355 °F/180 °C.

2. Let the brioche cool completely. To hollow out the brioche, insert a sharp knife into the top about ¾ in/2 cm from the edge and carve a circle around the top of the brioche, cutting diagonally down and toward the center and leaving about an inch on the bottom. Remove the cut-out portion carefully.

Fruit Medley

3. Prepare the pastry cream as described in the basic recipe, substituting the ingredients listed above. When cool, spread the cream on the inside of the brioche.

4. Arrange the fruit artistically on the pastry cream, inside the brioche. Decorate the top with a few mint leaves. To serve, cut the brioche into 6 portions and add a little pastry cream to each dish if there is any left over.

Aunt Odile's

For the brioche:
(see basic recipe)
½ cup/120 ml milk
2 tbsp/30 g sugar
1 oz/25 g compressed fresh yeast*
4 cups/500 g flour
4 eggs
5 tbsp/70 g brown sugar
½ cup/120 g butter
¾ cup/200 ml milk
a pinch of salt

For the vanilla custard:
(see basic recipe)
1 cup/250 ml milk
3 egg yolks
8 tsp/40 g sugar
1 vanilla bean

For the topping:
3 tbsp/50 g brown sugar
1 kiwano
1 pomegranate

Serves	*8*
Preparation time:	*1 hour 20 minutes*
Rining time:	*1 hour 20 minutes*
Cooking time:	*45 minutes*
Difficulty:	★ ★

Kiwano is a strange looking fruit with the shape of a kiwi, but covered by a hard shell with little spikes. These spikes give the kiwano its other common name, "horned melon." The green center is similar to that of a cucumber. Kiwano may also be cut in half lengthwise and eaten with a spoon, like an avocado, melon, or grapefruit.

Making brioche can be tricky, but as long as one scrupulously follows the instructions regarding the resting time of the dough, it should turn out as planned. It is very important that the yeast has time to work; however, if the dough is allowed to rest too long, the yeast may go sour and lend an unpleasant taste to the brioche. Brioche dough is very soft and may seem difficult to handle. Simply sprinkle a little flour on the board and on

your hands when kneading the dough. A large bundt pan works very nicely for forming and baking this brioche. The pan should be filled two-thirds full to allow the brioche to rise adequately as it bakes. The dough also needs a warm environment to rise properly. If your kitchen is too cool, our chef suggests placing the pan containing the dough over a larger pan with hot water.

One of the most convenient aspects of this recipe is that it allows for the use of a great variety of fruits. Any fruit with similar consistency may be used. This brioche is particularly appealing when served along with a custard.

*In hot climates and tropical regions, active dry yeast should be substituted for the compressed fresh yeast, halving the amount.

1. To make the brioche, warm ½ cup/120 ml milk and combine with 2 tbsp sugar in a ramekin or other small bowl. Crumble the yeast, then add it to the warm milk and sugar along with 6½ tbsp of the flour. Stir well and let rest for 20 minutes in a warm place.

2. In a large bowl, make a well in the remaining flour. Add the eggs, salt, brown sugar, softened butter and the rest of the milk. Once blended, add the yeast mixture. Stir well. The dough will be soft and shapeless. Cover with a cloth and let rise for 30 minutes.

Brioche

3. Scoop out the pomegranate and the kiwano and drain the fruit in a strainer. Prepare a vanilla custard as described in the basic recipe, substituting the ingredients listed above.

4. Fit the brioche dough by hand in a buttered pan. Cover with a cloth and let rest for 30 minutes. Decorate the top of the brioche with the fruit and sprinkle with the brown sugar. Bake for 30 minutes at 390 °F/200 °C, then lower the heat to 355 °F/180 °C for another 15 minutes.

Creole

1 tsp/ 5 g compressed fresh yeast*
1–2 tbsp/15–30 ml milk
1¼ cups/150 g flour
½ cup/120 g sugar
a pinch of salt

2 tbsp/30 g butter
3 eggs
2 tbsp white rum
1 lb/500 g litchis
1 oz/30 g guava gelatin

Serves	6
Preparation time:	25 minutes
Resting time:	30 minutes
Cooking time:	30–40 minutes
Difficulty:	★

There is a huge variety of bread pans and other forms to choose from, but for this recipe, our chef has chosen a basic pie pan for its simplicity. It is round, with edges of a suitable height and some even have a detachable bottom to facilitate removal of the brioche. To prevent the brioche from sticking, our chef suggests buttering and flouring the pan. This creates a thin film which protects the bread and allows it to be easily unmolded.

Brioche dough is difficult to handle because of its consistency. Regardless of the amount of butter and eggs, which will affect the thickness of the dough, it will always be fairly sticky and troublesome. Either compressed fresh yeast or active dry yeast can be used. If the active dry yeast is used, substitute one or two tablespoons of cold water for the warmed milk.

Litchis have a delicately sweet flavor, a rose-like taste that is well complimented by their juicy consistency. They will both moisten and sweeten the brioche. They may be difficult to find in regular supermarkets, but specialty stores or Asian markets almost always carry them. They are often found pitted and preserved in syrup. Guava gelatin may be found in the Hispanic foods section of many supermarkets.

Variations of this brioche include the addition of raisins or diced pineapple sprinkled with vanilla.

*In hot climates and tropical regions, active dry yeast should be substituted for the compressed fresh yeast, halving the amount.

1. Warm the milk and dissolve the yeast in it. Let this rest a few minutes. Sift the flour, sugar and salt into a large bowl. Stir in the yeast mixture.

2. Melt the butter. Add the eggs and melted butter, then the rum. Stir well until the dough becomes smooth and soft. Pour the dough into a buttered and floured pan and let rest at room temperature for 30 minutes.

Litchi Brioche

3. Peel and pit the litchis. Once pitted, reassemble them into their original shape.

4. Place the litchis in a decorative pattern on top of the brioche. Do not press them into the dough; they will sink in as the brioche bakes. Bake at 355 °F/180 °C for 30–40 minutes depending on the thickness of the brioche. Unmold while warm, then delicately brush on the guava gelatin. Serve warm or cold.

Persimmon

For the shortbread:
(see basic recipe)
1⅔ cups/200 g flour
6½ tbsp/100 g butter
a pinch of salt
3 tbsp water

For the filling:
⅓ cup/50 g cornstarch
1 cup/250 ml water

2 tbsp white rum
2 tbsp lemon juice
6 tbsp/90 g sugar
2 sheets of gelatin
3 persimmons
6½ tbsp/100 ml whipping cream

For the garnish:
a few leaves of fresh mint
1 persimmon

Serves | 6
Preparation time: | 50 minutes
Cooking time: | 35 minutes
Chilling time: | 1 hour 30 minutes
Difficulty: | ★

Persimmons are a wonderful fruit which bring a touch of originality to any dessert. There are two kinds of persimmon, the Japanese persimmon Hachiya, and the regular Fuyu persimmon which is more difficult to find in North America. Either variety of persimmon may be used for this pie. Despite its more acidic taste, mangos can be used here with great success.

Persimmons require delicate handling. If they are not ripe enough to peel or mash, they can be put in a food processor. Then simply strain the purée to remove any pieces of skin. The purée will be thickened later with the help of the gelatin, which will give the necessary body to the cream. For best results, the whipping cream should be very cold. It is also extremely important to add the whipped cream to the persimmon purée before the gelatin sets.

The decoration of this pie demands that the persimmons be cut very carefully and precisely. The persimmon quarters will look beautiful with a perfect sprig of mint. Mint can be kept fresh for several days by following our chef's suggestion: First, rinse and dry the mint. Then wrap it in a paper towel and keep it in the refrigerator in an airtight container. You will have fresh mint to use in tea, recipes, or as a garnish.

1. Stir the cornstarch into the water. Place over low heat and whisk until a very smooth cream forms. Make the shortbread according to the basic recipe but substituting the ingredients listed above, and let the dough rest for 30 minutes. Roll it out and ease it into a square pan. Prick it with a fork. Prebake it twice, at 390 °F/200 °C, for 15 minutes each time.

2. Stir the rum into the cornstarch cream, then add the lemon juice and 5 tbsp/75 g sugar. Let this thicken over low heat, then remove and let cool. In a small bowl, dissolve the gelatin in cold water, and stir the mixture into the cream.

Cream Pie

3. Peel the persimmons. Slice them, saving 6 of the nicest slices for the garnish. Purée the rest of the persimmons. Add the cream mixture to the puréed fruit. In a separate, chilled bowl, whip the whipping cream with the remaining sugar. Fold it into the persimmon purée.

4. Immediately fill the baked crust with the persimmon cream. Decorate the top with the 6 slices of persimmon and the mint leaves. Refrigerate for at least 1½ hours before serving.

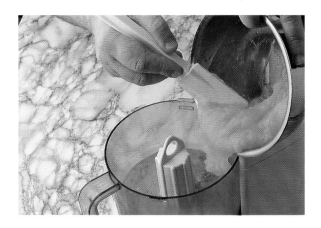

Chestnut and

20 ladyfingers

For the filling:
1 lb/500 g chestnuts
1¼ cups/300 g sugar
2½ cups/600 ml water
4 egg yolks
1 vanilla bean
2 sheets of gelatin
⅔ cup/150 ml heavy cream
7 oz/200 g strawberries

For the syrup for soaking:
¾ cup/200 ml water
6½ tbsp/100 g sugar
6½ tbsp/100 ml litchi liqueur

For the garnish:
a few leaves of fresh mint
10 large strawberries

Serves	*6*
Preparation time:	*1 hour*
Cooking time:	*30 minutes*
Chilling time:	*1 hour 30 minutes*
Difficulty:	★ ★

The origins of the charlotte, a sponge cake or ladyfinger-lined, molded dessert filled with cream, are not well documented. The harlotte is probably named after the wife of an English king who ruled at the end of the 18th century, and the dessert appears to have an English influence.

This recipe will enthrall anyone with a sweet tooth. But it is so delicious that it will please any guest, sweet tooth or not!

Certain important steps must be followed strictly in order for the charlotte to turn out as anticipated. After boiling the chestnuts, all the skin must be removed, for it is very bitter and can ruin the whole dessert. Also, if at all possible, purée the chestnuts in a food mill rather than a food processor. The food processor will tend to overprocess the chestnuts and give them a consistency that will not allow the filling to set properly. Of course, any other red fruits may be substituted equally well for the strawberries.

To allow for easier unmolding, run a warm, wet knife between the edge of the charlotte and the mold. If this dessert will be served to children, simply substitute fruit juice concentrate for the rum.

When serving this Chestnut and Strawberry Charlotte to guests, a strawberry coulis makes a very attractive and tasteful accompaniment. You will find that this is the perfect dessert after a spicy meal.

1. For the filling, peel the chestnuts, then boil them for 30 minutes in a syrup made from the sugar and the water. Remove the thin skin from the chestnuts. Purée them and stir in the egg yolks.

2. Add the vanilla bean to the purée. In a separate bowl, dissolve the gelatin in cold water and stir into the purée. In a chilled bowl, whip the cream, then fold it into the purée as well.

Strawberry Charlotte

3. Cut a few strawberries and place them in a flower shape on the bottom of the mold. Prepare the syrup for soaking with the water, sugar and litchi liqueur. Lightly soak the ladyfingers in the syrup, without letting them become soggy and line the mold with them.

4. Pour the chestnut purée into the mold and refrigerate for 1½ hours. Unmold to a platter and garnish with a little mint and some sliced strawberries around the base of the cake. Serve cool.

White Sapote

8¾ oz/250 g white sapotes
8¾ oz/250 g pink guava
1¼ cups/150 g flour
6 eggs
1 tsp nutmeg
zest of 1 lime
½ cup plus 2 tbsp/150 g sugar
2 cups/500 ml milk
1 tbsp butter

Serves   6
Preparation time: 30 minutes
Cooking time: 30 minutes
Difficulty: ★

Clafouti is a traditional French dessert consisting of fresh fruit and batter, which is both delicious and easy to prepare. With the exotic undertones of white sapote, this clafouti would make a very special birthday cake.

Guava and white sapote create a unique combination of flavors. Guava is reminiscent of peach and strawberries while the flesh of the white sapote is like that of apricots. Soak the fruit in a few tablespoons of alcohol, such as rum or Triple Sec, to enhance the flavor. Drain them well before adding them to the clafouti.

For an interesting variation in the flavor of this classic dessert, cinnamon may be substituted for the nutmeg. You will want the attractive colors and textures of the fruit to show on the surface of the clafouti. Our chef suggests first spreading a portion of the batter on the bottom of the pan, baking briefly to just set the batter, then adding the remaining batter before sprinkling with the fruit.

Because of its light consistency, the clafouti may rise above the edges of the pan toward the end of the baking. In this case, place a heavy cookie sheet on top of the clafouti while it cools. Since it should be served warm, this trick may also be done while rewarming the desert.

Clafouti is served in its baking pan, so it is important to choose an attractive one.

1. Peel and dice the fruit.

2. In a large bowl, combine the flour, eggs, nutmeg and the zest of lime. Slowly add the sugar and milk alternately.

Clafouti

3. Butter and lightly flour the baking pan. Pour the batter in the pan.

4. Sprinkle the fruit over the batter and allow it to sink in. Bake for 30 minutes at 355 °F/180 °C. Serve warm.

Asian Pear and

½ cup/75 g dried figs
½ cup/ 75 g dried dates
½ cup/120 ml white rum
8¾ oz/250 g Asian pears
⅓-½ cup/50 g nuts
⅓ cup/80 ml raisins

For the clafouti batter:
4 eggs
½ cup/125 g sugar
a pinch of salt
⅔ cup/80 g flour
⅓ cup/80 g butter
1 cup/250 ml milk
1 vanilla bean

Serves 4
Preparation time: 20 minutes
Cooking time: 20 minutes
Difficulty: ★

Clafouti is a type of fruit flan and derives its name from the patois verb *clafir* meaning "to fill." The traditional clafouti originates from the Limousin region of France, and consists of a thick crêpe batter baked with black cherries.

In this recipe, the clafouti is prepared in individual servings. It is generally eaten warm, but when prepared in a large pan, it is best to serve it cold. This will make it easier to cut and serve. If a large pan is used, the baking time should be increased by about twenty minutes.

Our chef has chosen a particularly pleasant combination of fruit. What child will not be thrilled to discover figs and dates stuffed with nuts for dessert? These fruit are often used in the traditional cuisine of Asian countries, particularly in the form of doughnuts, nougat and jams. Sifting the flour over the eggs will prevent lumping. If lumps do appear, simply run the batter through a food processor or blender in order to have a smooth finished product.

The vanilla bean can be replaced with cinnamon or orange zest. However, lemon zest should be avoided because it will curdle the milk.

1. Dice the fruit and macerate the dates and figs in the rum for 10 minutes. Add the Asian pears to the rum and let the fruit soak for another 30 minutes. At the last minute, strain the fruit and add the crushed nuts.

2. To make the batter, beat the eggs with the sugar and a pinch of salt. Sift the flour over the egg mixture and beat well.

Dried Fruit Clafouti

3. Melt the butter and then let it cool until it begins to harden. Add it to the egg mixture along with the milk and the seeds from the vanilla bean.

4. Butter individual ramekins. Spoon the strained fruit into each dish and pour the clafouti batter over the fruit. Sprinkle a few raisins on each one. Bake at 355 °F/180 °C for 20 minutes. Dust with confectioners' sugar and serve.

Pineapple

For the lightly leavened dough:
   (see basic recipe)
¼ cup/65 g butter
½ cup/125 ml milk
1 tbsp/15 g compressed fresh yeast*
1⅔ cups/200 g flour
5 tbsp/70 g sugar
zest of 1 orange
1 egg yolk
a pinch of salt

1 pineapple

For the garnish:
5 tbsp/70 g confectioners' sugar

Serves   6
Preparation time: 30 minutes
Rising time;   30 minutes
Cooking time: 40 minutes
Difficulty: ★

Pineapple, a majestic-looking fruit, can be found in the simplest of desserts. When pineapple was first introduced into Europe, it was completely ignored. No one wanted to buy this green fruit which always seemed unripe; in fact the darker color of today's pineapple was in fact artificially created to make it appear more appetizing! This fruit is overflowing with vitamins and even contains an enzyme which aids digestion. The appearance of uncut pineapples may vary, but the varieties all look the same when cut. Pineapples will continue to ripen when stored at room temperature. For this recipe, a soft pineapple should be chosen, with green leaves and a strong aroma.

Because this recipe uses a yeast dough, two factors should be taken into consideration: the room temperature and the timing of the resting periods. To keep the dough uniform, spoon it into the bundt pan, then tap the pan against the counter to allow any bubbles or holes to disappear. This will prevent unsightly cavities from appearing while the dough bakes. This dessert is particularly delicious when it is served warm and accompanied by a custard flavored with coconut liqueur or with vanilla. The combination of these two flavors is particularly enticing. Serve this cake with the pineapple on the top, or for a pleasant surprise, serve it as an upside-down cake.

*In hot climates and tropical regions, active dry yeast should be substituted for the compressed fresh yeast, halving the amount.

1. Prepare a lightly leavened dough: Melt 1 tbsp butter, warm the milk, then combine the warm milk and yeast with the melted butter. Pour this into the flour, then add the sugar, salt and the remaining butter. Stir in the orange zest and the egg yolk. Knead the dough well and let rise for 30 minutes.

2. Prepare the pineapple by cutting off both ends. Peel, and be sure to remove all the black spikes. Dice the fruit.

Crown

3. Spoon the dough into a bundt pan. Place the diced pineapple on the dough. Bake for 40 minutes at 355 °F/180 °C.

4. Unmold while still warm and sprinkle with confectioners' sugar so that the pineapple absorbs it and only the sugar on the cake is visible.

For the passion fruit sauce:
⅔ cup/150 ml passion fruit juice
⅔ cup/150 ml sugar syrup (see basic recipe)
2 tsp/10 ml honey

For the caramel:
6½ tbsp/100 g butter
6½ tbsp/100 g sugar
6½ tbsp/100 g brown sugar
6½ tbsp/100 ml orange juice
⅓ cup/40 g flour

For the cream cheese filling:
3 tbsp water
½ cup/120 g sugar
3 egg yolks
4 sheets of gelatin
4 kiwi
14 oz/400 g cream cheese
1 cup/250 ml heavy cream

For the garnish:
a few fresh mint leaves
confectioners' sugar

Serves	*6*
Preparation time:	*1 hour*
Cooking time:	*10 minutes*
Chilling time:	*2 hours*
Difficulty:	★ ★

This elegant dessert is presented here in all its glory. However, it can also be made in individual servings. For a variation in the texture, consider adding chopped almonds to the cake to give it even more crunch.

The most critical part of the preparation of this recipe is baking the caramel. One must not leave the kitchen after it has been put in the oven, for it needs constant supervision. If the caramel is closely monitored, however, it will not have a chance to accidentally blacken or burn.

After removing the caramel disks from the oven, let them cool completely before attempting to remove them from the baking sheet. If it is even slightly warm, the caramel will be soft enough to bend and this will ruin the shape of the layer.

Low-fat cream cheese can be used in this recipe, which may be a consideration in choosing a dessert. Knowing that this cheesecake recipe is also low-fat makes it twice as enjoyable. The kiwi can be replaced with mango for variety's sake.

One recommendation: The cream and cream cheese should not be overbeaten when preparing the batter. This will prevent the cream from becoming too stiff to spread the it on the caramel disks.

The passion fruit sauce lends the perfect tang to this creamy cake. However, if mango is used in the cake, prepare the sauce with mangoes as well.

1. Prepare the passion fruit sauce by warming the passion fruit juice over low heat with the syrup. Add the honey. Stir well, then remove from heat and let cool. Prepare the caramel by melting the butter and combining it with the sugars. Stir in the orange juice and flour.

2. Form 3 disks by spreading the caramel on parchment paper on a cookie sheet. Bake at 340 °F/170 °C or 355 °F/180 °C for about 10 minutes until the caramel darkens. Let the disks cool completely and trim them so that they are identical in size and shape. Set aside. Begin preparing the filling by bringing the water and sugar to a boil.

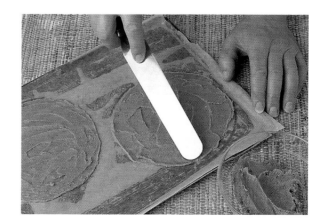

Caramel Cheesecake

3. Beat the egg yolks into the sugar syrup. Melt the gelatin and stir it into the mixture. Peel and dice the kiwi, and blend them in along with the cream cheese. Whip the heavy cream and fold it into the cream cheese and fruit mixture. Place 1 caramel disk in the bottom of a high-edged cake pan. Cover with about half the cream cheese filling.

4. Place the second disk on the cream cheese and spread it with the remaining cream cheese mixture. Place the last caramel disk on top. Using a grill for the pattern, sprinkle confectioners' sugar over the cake. Refrigerate for 2 hours before serving.

For the craquelin:
½ cup/120 g butter
½ cup plus 2 tbsp/150 g sugar
7 tbsp/50 g corn sugar or dextrose
1¼ cup/170 g slivered almonds

For the pastry cream:
1 cup/250 ml milk
1 vanilla bean
3½ tbsp/50 g sugar
4 tsp/10 g flour
4 tsp/10 g cornstarch
2 egg yolks
3½ tbsp/50 ml orange-flavored liqueur

For the filling:
2 Asian pears
juice of 1 lemon
2 tbsp/30 g butter
3½ tbsp/50 g sugar

Serves	4
Preparation time:	1 hour
Cooking time:	1 hour
Chilling time:	1 hour 30 minutes
Difficulty:	★ ★

The type of caramel used in this recipe is called *craquelin*. It is commonly used in traditional French bakeries in light and crispy petit fours, or in unsweetened cakes. Craquelin is also often served with ice cream and custard.

Our chef's almond caramel craquelin is particularly crunchy, and can easily withstand the juiciness of the pears. Shaping the craquelin is the most delicate part of this recipe: The caramel must still be warm so that it can be shaped and properly fitted into the pan. As it bakes, it has a tendency to darken rapidly and burn easily, so it is important to monitored it closely as soon as it is put in the oven. Our chef suggests basting them with the

juice they yield as they bake. This will give them an even and attractive color. Using the point of a paring knife is the best way to tell when the pears are done. They will pierce easily when they are ready.

The slivered almonds can be replaced with other nuts, pistachios for example. A mixture of several varieties of nuts is also a good variation. If regular pears are are substituted for the Asian pears, they should be just barely ripe, and the baking time should be cut in half. Broil for the last minute to brown.

The craquelin should be served very fresh.

1. Prepare the craquelin by thoroughly combining the butter, sugar, corn sugar and almonds. Make the pastry cream as explained in the basic recipes but substituting the ingredients listed above. Refrigerate it for at least 1 hour.

2. Thinly roll out the craquelin and place it on a buttered or nonstick cookie sheet. Bake at 430 °F/220 °C for 10 minutes. When removing the craquelin from the oven, peel it off of the cookie sheet and ease it into a pan, shaping it into the form of your choice. Save the excess craquelin for the garnish.

Asian Pears

3. Peel and seed the pears. Squeeze a little lemon juice over them to prevent them from turning brown. Cut them in half and place them cut-side down in a baking dish with the butter and sugar. Bake at 430 °F/220 °C for 40–50 minutes, then broil to caramelize the top.

4. Spread the pastry cream on the bottom of the shaped craquelin. Let the pears cool for at least 30 minutes, then carefully place the pears on the pastry cream and decorate with extra craquelin.

Vishnou

For the short pastry:
(see basic recipe)
1⅔ cups/200 g flour
6½ tbsp/100 g butter
1 egg
2 tbsp water
a pinch of salt

For the filling:
8¾ oz/250 g tamarind or Indian date
1 cup/150 g dried dates
1 cup/100 g walnuts
2 eggs
1 tbsp/15 g butter
1 tbsp very strong tea
3 tbsp/45 g sugar
¾ cup plus 1 tbsp/100 g flour
¾ cup/175 ml milk
½ packet of yeast

Serves	*4*
Preparation time:	*35 minutes*
Cooking time:	*55 minutes*
Resting time:	*30 minutes*
Difficulty:	★ ★

Tamarind, the fruit of the tamarind tree, resembles a small sausage both in color and shape.

Tamarind pulp is sweet but quite tart and contains tiny, hard seeds. It is also known as the Indian date, and is often used to make jam, sorbets, chutneys and a variety of beverages. In this recipe, our chef has combined the flavors of the tamarind with those of dates and walnuts.

Our chef notes that removing the pulp from the tamarind is a slow process, and that they must be soaked in water overnight before using them. Stir the fruit in the water before removing them so that the skin and other debris are easily removed. If time is short, do not use tamarinds in this recipe. Substitute dates and nuts or even dried figs and cashews for the tamarinds.

To decorate these little tarts, half a date can be placed on the filling as it is baking. However, the dates should not be added before the filling has had time to set or they will sink and serve no decorative purpose! After the croustades have cooled somewhat, cut a stencil of your choice out of paper and sprinkle confectioners' sugar over each one for the finishing touch.

This dessert will be a perfect morsel to serve at tea or to end a good meal.

1. Make a short pastry as explained in the basic recipe using the ingredients listed above. Let it rest 30 minutes, then roll out the pastry and ease it into 4 individual buttered tart pans. Prebake twice at 390 °F/200 °C, for 15 minutes each time, and allow to cool. Slice the soaked tamarinds and scoop out the pulp. Remove the seeds. Cut the dates into small pieces and crush the walnuts.

2. Beat the eggs and melt the butter, then combine them with the tea, sugar, flour, milk and half of the yeast. Beat the batter until there are no lumps and it is perfectly smooth.

Croustade

3. In a small bowl, combine the tamarind, dates and nuts. Divide this mixture into the 4 tart shells.

4. Cover each portion carefully with the batter. Bake at 355 °F/180 °C for 20–25 minutes. After about 15 minutes, place a date or nut on top of the dough for decoration. Unmold while still warm.

Coffee Croustade

For the sweet short pastry:
(see basic recipe)
1⅔ cups/200 g flour
6½ tbsp/100 g sugar
6½ tbsp/100 g butter
2 eggs
a pinch of salt

For the coffee filling:
3½ tbsp/50 g sugar
⅔ cup/150 ml whipping cream
3 egg yolks
1 tbsp instant coffee

For the garnish:
12¼ oz/350 g finger bananas
6½ tbsp/100 ml rum

Serves	*4*
Preparation time:	*40 minutes*
Cooking time:	*20 minutes*
Chilling time:	*1 hour*
Difficulty:	*★*

For many years banana trees served as attractive garden plants, making them almost more popular for their appearance than for their fruit. But times have changed! Bananas are now readily available around the world and are easily exported.

There are two basic types of bananas. The first is the familiar banana, which is commonly eaten raw or cooked, as a snack or in desserts. The plantain is much larger and is almost always served cooked as a vegetable. Bananas are rich in potassium and very nourishing. Of the varieties of bananas commonly found in the supermarket, the most familiar is the farge banana, which has a soft consistency when ripe. However, for recipes such as this in which the bananas are baked, our chef recommends the dwarf or finger banana, often marketed as "baby bananas."

They tend to retain their firmness when cooked better than the standard banana.

The coffee filling does not require whipping, which would give it too smooth a consistency. Instant coffee adds a pleasant zing to the filling and also serves as a coloring, which will provide a good contrast with the light pastry. However, it must be watched closely while baking so that it does not darken too sharply. To prevent overbrowning, consider protecting the little tarts with tin foil. If your oven allows, change the oven setting so that the heat only comes from underneath. It is important that the pastry be properly cooked. Let your imagination run wild when decorating these croustades. Confectioners' sugar and extra banana slices will make a fitting garnish.

1. Make the short sweet pastry as described in the basic recipe but substituting the ingredients listed above, and let it rest for 30 minutes. Roll it out and prick it with a fork. Ease the pastry into 4 buttered and floured individual-sized tart pans.

2. Slice the bananas and macerate them in the rum.

with Finger Bananas

3. Fill each tart shell with marinated banana slices.

4. Combine the sugar, whipping cream, egg yolks and coffee. Stir until the coffee is totally dissolved. Cover the bananas with the coffee filling. Bake for 20 minutes at 355 °F/180 °C. Refrigerate for 1 hour before serving.

Souffléed Rice and

For the filling:
4 tbsp white rice
½ cup/120 ml milk
3½ tbsp/50 g butter
6½ tbsp/100 g sugar
2 tbsp white rum
4 eggs, separated
8¾ oz/250 g pineapple
1 combava

For the shortbread:
(see basic recipe)
2 cups/250 g flour
½ cup/125 g butter
3 tbsp milk or water
a pinch of salt
½ cup/125 g sugar

Serves	*6*
Preparation time:	*1 hour*
Cooking time:	*35 minutes*
Difficulty:	★ ★ ★

Rice has a long and exciting history. Before reaching the West, rice traveled from China, through southeast Asia to the Middle East, where sophisticated irrigation techniques were developed. Through colonization, as well as numerous invasions, rice was slowly exported and became popular around the world. Many different types of rice have been cultivated. Rice plays a significant role in Caribbean cuisine.

In this recipe it is not necessary to use the best quality rice since it will be ground. The rice should be left to soak overnight. For convenience, rice flour may be substituted. Rice flour does not require soaking, but the amount of milk should be doubled. When the other ingredients are being combined with the rice, our chef recommends adding the eggs last. This will prevent the heat of the rice from cooking the eggs.

The zest of combava, a wild cousin of the lime, is used here as a spice. Not much is necessary as it is very strong. Lime may be used if combava is not available. Our chef suggest adding a little salt to the egg whites to help them form peaks. Also, all the little black "eyes" from the pineapple should be removed after peeling it. This will avoid the appearance of mysterious, crunchy, black prickles in the soufflé!

1. Soak the rice overnight. Purée the soaked rice in a food processor very finely. Prepare the shortbread pastry according to the directions in the basic recipe but substituting the ingredients listed above. Let it rest 30 minutes. Roll it out and then ease it into a flan or pie pan. Prebake it twice, for 10 minutes at 390 °F/200 °C each time.

2. Combine the rice purée and the milk, and cook over low heat until it thickens. Remove immediately before it burns.

Pineapple Croustade

3. Quickly beat in the butter, sugar, rum and then the egg yolks. Peel the pineapple and cut it into small pieces. Stir the pineapple and the combava zest into the filling mixture.

4. Whip the egg whites and fold them into the batter, then pour it into the crust. Bake at 375 °F/190 °C for 10 minutes, then at 445 °F/230 °C for 5 minutes. The pie is done when it develops a delicate golden brown color.

1 lb/500 g dried figs
¾ cup/175 ml dark rum
¾ cup/175 ml water
1 lb/500 g fresh figs
1 package of phyllo pastry or *feuille de brick* pastry
2 tbsp/30 g butter, melted

⅓ cup plus 1 tbsp/50 g slivered almonds
½ cup/50 g coarsely chopped pistachios
2 pinches of cinnamon
4 tsp/20 g sugar

Serves	6
Preparation time:	15 minutes
Cooking time:	17 minutes
Difficulty:	★

Fresh figs are very delicate and once ripe they will spoil rapidly, often within 24 hours. Types of figs are differentiated by their size, skin and flesh. When purchasing figs, whether white or purple, the thinner the skin the better.

Dried figs, which have a great deal of flavor, add a honey-like character which they acquire as they dry in the sun. If they are not marinated overnight, they should be soaked in warm water for at least 30 minutes before beginning this recipe.

For the marinade, rum is usually used, but other types of alcohol will work as well. Boukha, a fig-based spirit, will enhance the flavor of the fruit. The almonds and pistachio, in addition to adding their distinctive flavors, help to absorb some of the excess juice that the fruit will expel as it bakes. This will prevent the feuilleté from becoming soggy. The pistachios can be replaced by walnuts.

The phyllo pastry should be buttered before it is baked. Our chef suggests brick pastry, but this is not readily available in many areas, and phyllo is a fine substitute.

After baking, decorate the feuilleté with a row of sliced fresh figs. If desired, sprinkle with confectioners' sugar.

1. Quarter the dried figs, then macerate them in the rum and water overnight. Drain them before preparing the feuilleté.

2. Wash and thinly slice the fresh figs.

Dried Fig Feuilleté

3. Place the pastry in a buttered baking pan of your choice. Leave enough pastry extending over the edge of the pan to fold and cover the filling.

4. Place a layer of dried figs on the pastry, followed by a layer of pistachios and then almonds. Sprinkle with the sugar and cinnamon. Close the feuilleté and brush with the melted butter. Finish with a layer of fresh figs. Bake for 2 minutes at 390 °F/200 °C then 15 minutes at 320 °F/160 °C. Serve warm.

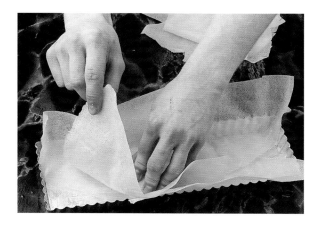

Orange

For the crumble:
2 cups/250 g flour
1 cup/125 g finely ground almonds
½ tsp powdered cinnamon
1 tsp/5 g salt
4 hard-boiled egg yolks
½ cup plus 3 tbsp/170 g butter
1 egg
½ cup/125 g brown sugar
2 tbsp/30 ml rum

For the orange marmalade:
5 oranges, diced
1¼ cups/300 g brown sugar
¾ cup/200 ml water

Serves | 6
Preparation time: | 30 minutes
Resting time: | 1 hour
Cooking time: | 1 hour 30 minutes
Difficulty: | ★

The success of tarts and pies lies in the quality of their crust. This crumble will showcase the talents of the baker.

The egg yolks and almonds will dry out the crumble and make it quite flaky. If it is so flaky as to become unmanageable, another raw egg should be added as a binder. The trick with crumble is that it cannot be rolled out, but must be pressed in the pan by hand and flattened with the fingers. Consequently, our chef suggests serving it in its pan without attempting to unmold it. Or for a more personal touch, the crumble can be served in individual-sized ramekins.

It is imperative that the oranges be stewed for at least one hour. If this recipe is being made at the last minute, the oranges can be thickened with extra almond powder. They can also be enhanced by adding a few drops of rum.

Leftover crumble tropping can be formed into cookies, which should be baked for about ten minutes. These are excellent served with tea, especially when accompanied with a fruit custard or an orange cream.

The effort put into preparing the crumble will be well rewarded by your guests' pleasure when enjoying this treat.

1. Combine the flour, almond powder, cinnamon and salt. Make a well in the dry ingredients and break up the hard boiled egg yolks in the center. Add the softened butter, egg, brown sugar and rum. Work these ingredients together by hand. Form into a ball and let it rest in the refrigerator for 1 hour.

2. In a buttered pan, press in a layer of crumble about ³⁄₁₆ in/5 mm thick. Break up the remaining crumble and set aside.

Crumble

3. Prepare the marmalade by combining the oranges, brown sugar and water. Let simmer for about 1 hour, until the oranges reach a soft, jam-like consistency. Spread the marmalade into the crumble crust.

4. Sprinkle the remaining crumble over the filling. Bake at 390 °F/200 °C for 30–35 minutes. Serve warm.

Ginger and

For the sweet short pastry:
   (see basic recipe)
1⅔ cups/200 g flour
6½ tbsp/100 g sugar
6½ tbsp/100 g butter
2 eggs
a pinch of salt

For the filling:
4 small avocados
juice of 1 lime
2 tbsp litchi liqueur
4 sheets of gelatin
½ cup water
6 tbsp ginger marmalade
¾ cup/200 ml heavy cream

Serves	*8*
Preparation time:	*45 minutes*
Cooking time:	*35 minutes*
Chilling time:	*1 hour*
Difficulty:	*★*

This is quite a unique dessert since both its flavor and its shape are out of the ordinary. The crust appears difficult to make, but in fact it is fairly simple to do. However, shortbread is delicate and must be handled with care. A pastry jagger, which is a pastry wheel with a fluted edge, is the best way to make the petal-shaped pieces. They will be overlapped around the edge of the pan, with one in the center to bind them all together. The pieces that overlap should be pressed together firmly so that they hold together as they bake. If necessary, a little egg yolk can be brushed on to help them adhere.

If extra flour is added to the pastry for ease of handling, any excess flour should be brushed away with a pastry brush before baking, for it will prevent the petals from sticking together properly. Note that this type of crust can only be used with fillings that do not need to be baked and which will not make the crust soggy.

The choice of avocado as the filling for this dessert is a surprise, since avocados are usually found in appetizers and main courses. However, the nutty flavor and smooth consistency of the avocado make it easily adaptable to pastries. The lime juice is vital to the success of this pie because it will prevent the avocado from oxidizing and turning black.

This surprising tart will enchant and surprise any guest.

1. Prepare the shortbread pastry as described in the basic recipe but substituting the ingredients listed above. Let it rest 30 minutes. Butter the pan before laying the pastry in it as described above. Prick the pastry with a fork. Prebake it twice at 390 °F/200 °C for 15 minutes each time.

2. Peel and quarter the avocados, and place them in a food processor with the lime juice and litchi liqueur. Mix well to develop a smooth purée.

Avocado Mousse Pie

3. Dissolve the gelatin in the water. Warm the ginger marmalade in a double boiler or water bath. Combine the gelatin and the marmalade. Separately, whip the cream and then fold it into the avocado. Stir in the jam. Refrigerate for 1 hour.

4. Fill the tart shell using a pastry bag with an appropriate tip.

Chocolate and Red

For the nougat:
1¾ oz/50 g dextrose
½ cup/120 g sugar
10 tbsp/150 g butter
1 cup/170 g slivered almonds

For the dark chocolate mousse:
3½ oz/100 g dark chocolate
3½ tbsp/50 g butter
3 eggs, separated
½ cup/40 g grated coconut

For the white chocolate mousse:
3½ oz/100 g white chocolate
3½ tbsp/50 g butter
3 egg yolks
1 tbsp vanilla sugar
6½ tbsp/100 ml heavy cream
3½ oz/100 g red currants

For the garnish:
1 oz/30 g dark chocolate
a few fresh mint leaves
a few red currants

Serves	*6*
Preparation time:	*1 hour 10 minutes*
Cooking time:	*10 minutes*
Chilling time:	*1 hour*
Difficulty:	★ ★

Red currants, attractive little berries that hang in clusters like grapes, are sometimes available in supermarkets. If currants are not available, raspberries, blackberries or even blueberries may be used. In the case of these substitutes, decorate the cake at the last minute or the color of the berries will seep into the mousse and leave unattractive blotches of color.

For a lighter dessert, the white chocolate mousse can be replaced by a simple whipped cream, incorporating the currants. In this case, the whipped cream will have to be very firm in order to withstand the weight of the nougat. When assembling the cake, the mousse should not be too cold or it will be very difficult to push through the pastry bag. However, it is essential that the finished *feuillantine* be refrigerated for at least one hour before being served, as it should be eaten very cold and the chocolate mousse will take a long time to chill.

The chocolate designs which decorate the feuillantine are fairly simple to make. Fill a pastry bag with melted chocolate and let your imagination run wild.

Any leftover red currants can be used for a garnish as well. This dessert should be served promptly after removing it from the refrigerator. If the mousse is allowed to warm, it will cause the nougat to absorb excess moisture and thus ruin the whole effect of this dessert.

1. Prepare the nougat by combining the dextrose, sugar, butter and almonds. Spread it out on a buttered nonstick cookie sheet. Bake for 8–10 minutes at 355 °F/180 °C until golden brown. Cut out 3 identical sheets of nougat using a bread pan or plastic container as a guideline.

2. For the dark chocolate mousse, melt the chocolate in a double boiler or in the microwave and soften the butter. Stir the softened butter, egg yolks and coconut into the melted chocolate. Let cool. Whip the egg whites and fold them into the chocolate mixture.

Currant Feuillantine

3. For the white chocolate mousse, melt the chocolate in a double boiler or in the microwave and soften the butter. Stir in the softened butter, egg yolks, vanilla and sugar. Whip the cream, fold it into the chocolate mixture, then gently stir in the red currants.

4. Using a pastry bag with a star tip, cover the first nougat sheet with the dark chocolate mousse. Lie the second sheet of nougat on the mousse and cover it with the white chocolate mousse. Place the last sheet of nougat on top and decorate it with melted chocolate, red currants and mint. Chill for 1 hour or more before serving.

Three Layer Rum

For the shortbread:
(see basic recipe)
4 cups/500 g flour
6½ tbsp/100 g sugar
1 cup/250 g butter
a pinch of salt
some water or 1 egg

For the pastry cream:
1 cup/250 ml milk
3½ tbsp/50 g sugar

2 egg yolks
1 vanilla bean
2 sheets of gelatin
½ cup/80 g raisins
6½ tbsp/100 ml white rum
⅔ cup/150 ml heavy cream

For the garnish:
confectioners' sugar
2 large strawberries
a few fresh mint leaves

Serves	6
Preparation time:	1 hour
Cooking time:	15 minutes
Chilling time:	3 hours
Difficulty:	★

Shortbread is the perfect crust for a pastry cream, despite its inconveniences, in particular the difficulty involved in rolling it out. It must also be prepared rapidly to prevent the butter from melting. The work space should be cool and lightly floured. If the dough breaks while rolling it out, flour should not be added, though this is often a temptation. Extra flour will not make it more manageable.

To prepare three tiers of the exact same shape and size, the edge of a springform pan can be used as a cookie cutter. If there is extra dough, it will make delightful cut-out cookies. They should be baked according to the same instructions detailed below. The caramelization which our chef suggests for the shortbread layers will allow them to become even more resistant to the pastry cream's moisture and will help the pastry retain its delicate crunchy texture. While traditional pastry cream does not contain gelatin, to be on the safe side, and to make sure that the pastry cream will be stiff enough to withstand the weight of the shortbread, our chef suggests using two sheets of gelatin.

The garnish of the strawberry grape vine, designed by our chef, was made with a tiny melon baller. The mint leaves, which should be carefully rinsed before being placed on the cake, make a clever vine. Of course, the strawberry grape vine is only a suggestion and can be omitted if there are time constraints.

1. Make a shortbread pastry as instructed in the basic recipe but substituting the ingredients listed above. Let it rest for 30 minutes. Roll it out and cut out 3 identical layers. Sprinkle them with confectioners' sugar so they caramelize when baked. Bake on a nonstick cookie sheet for 15 minutes at 390 °F/200 °C.

2. Make a pastry cream as instructed in the basic recipes, but adding the gelatin, which should be dissolved in a little water ahead of time. Reserve in the refrigerator for 30 minutes. Soak the raisins in the rum before beginning the pastry, then drain them and stir into the pastry cream.

Raisin Shortbread Cake

3. Whip the cream and fold it into the pastry cream. Refrigerate for 30 minutes.

4. Place the first shortbread layer in a springform pan. Spread some of the cream on the layer. Place the second layer on the cream and repeat. Finish with the third layer. Refrigerate for 2 hours. Sprinkle with confectioners' sugar and garnish with the strawberries and mint.

Surelle and Pink

For the puff pastry: (see basic recipe or use packaged puff pastry)
1⅔ cups/200 g flour
½ cup/125 g butter
1 cup/250 ml water
2 tbsp sugar
4 medium eggs
2 pinches of salt

For the filling:
1¾ oz/50 g surelles
3½ oz/100 g pink pralines
⅓ cup/80 g butter
2 tbsp/sugar
1 egg
⅓ cup/40 g finely chopped almonds
½ cup/40 g grated coconut
1 tbsp dark rum
1 tbsp flour

Serves	6
Preparation time:	45 minutes
Cooking time:	30 minutes
Difficulty:	★

Surelles are a fruit which resemble tiny, pale green apples and have a mildly tart flavor which contrasts well with the almonds and pink pralines. In this case, the pralines consist of candy-coated almonds. If pink pralines are not available, they can be replaced with sugar-coated peanuts.

Almond liqueur or a few drops of orange blossom water are both acceptable substitutes for the rum. This dessert can be made a day in advance, but in that case, the feuilleté must be well-sealed and refrigerated until immediately before baking so that it remains fresh. It is imperative that the cookie sheet or wax paper used be lightly moistened to prevent the pastry from sticking to it. One interesting option is to prepare the feuilleté in individual sizes and serve it with almond ice cream.

The tip of a sharp knife can be used to score decorative designs in the pastry before brushing it with egg yolk and baking it. For a finishing touch, three surelles or pink pralines can be used to decorate the feuilleté. Here they are placed right on top of the "chimney" of the pastry.

This creative dessert should be served warm.

1. Prepare the puff pastry as instructed in the basic recipe but substituting the ingredients listed above. Let it rest for 30 minutes, then roll it out to a thickness of ⅛ in/3 mm. Cut 2 identical triangles out of the pastry. The edges of the triangles should be about 10 in/25 cm long. Place 1 triangle on a damp cookie sheet and set the other aside.

2. Pit the surelles and set them aside. Coarsely crush the pink pralines in a bowl with a pestle. Save 3 whole pralines to decorate the pastry.

Praline Feuilleté

3. Soften the butter and add it to the crushed pralines along with the sugar, egg, chopped almonds, coconut, rum and flour. Stir until the mixture is well blended and light in color.

4. Spread this almond cream on the first pastry triangle. Scatter the pitted surelles over the cream. Seal the pastry with the second triangle, brushing egg yolk between the edges. Brush beaten egg yolk over the top as well. Pierce a small hole in the center, and bake at 430 °F/220 °C for 5 minutes, then at 390 °F/200 °C for 25 minutes.

Grapefruit and

1 large pink grapefruit
3½ tbsp/50 g butter
3½ tbsp/50 g sugar
3½ tbsp/50 ml white rum
2 pinches of curry powder
1 egg

For the short pastry:
  (see basic recipe)
1 cup/120 g flour
1 egg
a pinch of salt
3½ tbsp/50 g sugar
¼ cup/60 g butter

For the puff pastry:
  (see basic recipe)
½ cup/120 g butter
1¼ cups/150 g flour
5 tbsp/75 ml water
a pinch of salt

Serves	6
Preparation time:	1 hour
Cooking time:	1 hour
Chilling time:	1 hour 30 minutes
Difficulty:	★

Many fruits can be used instead of grapefruit in this recipe. Pomelo, which is very similar to grapefruit, and mandarin oranges are suitable replacements. If grapefruit is used, pink grapefruit has the tenderest pulp. This recipe will please any citrus-lover, especially when combined with the two sweet pastries our chef has chosen.

Ground cardamom can replace the curry if necessary. When curry was first developed, each region of India had its own variation, with many possible ingredients. In 1889 an official recipe was developed which included clove, coriander, fenugreek, turmeric and cardamom. The complex flavors of curry will give this dessert a sophisticated taste. The short pastry should be pricked with a fork once it has been fitted into the pan. This will prevent it from rising when it bakes. Use the pie pan as a cookie cutter to make the top crust of the pie. This technique will ensure a perfect fit.

The top layer can be larger than the pan, to aid in sealing. The egg will bind the pastry layers together. It also should be used to brush the top of the pie to give it color as it bakes. Thanks to the "chimney," the juices will be able to evaporate and will not make the bottom crust soggy. With a set of attractive cookie cutters and some of the puff pastry, children can be kept entertained making the garnish for the top of the pie while the rest of the recipe is being prepared.

1. Dice the whole grapefruit (peel and all), reserving the juice. Very lightly sauté the grapefruit with the butter, sugar and rum so that it cooks but does not caramelize (about 40 minutes). Little by little, stir in the reserved juice.

2. Near the end of the sautéing, add the curry. Prepare the short pastry as described in the basic recipe but substituting the ingredients listed above. Butter a pie pan and fit the short pastry into it. Prepare the puff pastry as described in the basic recipe, again using the ingredients listed above.

Curry Pie

3. Fill the pie with the curried grapefruit and lay on the top crust of the puff pastry, using the egg to seal the 2 crusts together. Make a "chimney" in the center to allow steam to escape, and brush the remaining egg on the top crust.

4. Decorate the top crust with additional puff pastry shapes. Bake for 1 hour at 390 °F/200 °C. When done, refrigerate for at least 1½ hours and serve cold.

Charlotte

20 ladyfingers
1 large, flat almond meringue or 1 layer of
    sponge cake (see basic recipes for both)

For the syrup:
2¾ cups/700 ml water
3½ tbsp/50 g sugar
juice of 1 lime
⅔ cup/150 ml white rum

For the filling:
2 kiwi
1 mango
12 strawberries
1 small pineapple
1 orange
4½ tbsp/100 g apricot jam

Serves   6
Preparation time: 1 hour
Cooking time: 5 minutes
Chilling time: 1 hour
Difficulty: ★ ★

For the pastry cream:
¼ cup/50 g passion fruit
½ cup/100 g strawberries
1 banana
1 mango
1 lime
4 egg yolks
3½ tbsp/50 g sugar
2 tbsp/15 g cornstarch
2 sheets of gelatin
4½ tbsp/70 g butter
1 cup/250 ml heavy cream

For the garnish:
a few leaves of fresh mint

One of the secrets of a successful charlotte lies in the handling of the ladyfingers. They should not be soaked in the syrup for too long or they will become soggy and lose their shape.

Children will love this dessert, but of course the rum should be replaced by a non-alcoholic flavoring such as fruit juice. Use a base of almond meringue or sponge cake as described in the basic recipes, or on a pinch, a bought sponge layer.

The pastry cream is based on a standard pastry cream, but is unusual in that it calling for fruit juice rather than milk as the required liquid. The fruit listed here can be used or others can be added. Another possibility is to use only fruit juice in the cream rather than the fruit pulp.

In the interest of time, the fruit can be mixed in with the pastry cream. Our chef warns against using overripe fruit. To give the charlotte a professional look and additional flavor, consider adding a thin layer of guava jelly or other fruit jelly.

This dessert should be served cold, but cannot be frozen or the consistency of the pastry cream will be ruined.

1. Line the bottom of a mold with the almond meringue or sponge layer. Prepare the syrup by dissolving the sugar in 3½ tbsp/50 ml water and bringing it to a boil. Stir in the lime juice, rum and rest of the water. Lightly soak the ladyfingers in the syrup and line the edges of a mold with them.

2. Peel and dice the fruit for the filling Strain the fruit for the pastry cream, retaining the juice.

Tropicana

3. For the pastry cream, bring the fruit juice to a boil. Whisk the egg yolks with the sugar in a double boiler. Stir in the cornstarch and then pour in the hot juice. Bring this to a boil. In a separate bowl, dissolve the gelatin in cold water. Combine it with the hot juice and add the butter, then let cool and fold it in.

4. Cover the meringue or sponge base with the pastry cream. Add a layer of the diced fruit, then the rest of the cream, and decoratively top it with the remaining fruit. Refrigerate for 1 hour. Brush with apricot jam or guava jelly and garnish with mint leaves.

For the filling:
1 medium orange
6½ tbsp/100 g sugar
½ cup water

For the batter:
7 oz/200 g dark chocolate
13 tbsp/200 g butter
4 eggs
¾ cup plus 1 tbsp/200 g sugar

1⅔ cups/200 g flour
a pinch of salt
1 vanilla bean
¾ cup/ 200 ml whipping cream
2 pinches curry powder

For the garnish:
⅓ cup/50 g confectioners' sugar
3 orange slices

Serves 6
Preparation time: 30 minutes
Cooking time: 30 minutes
Difficulty: ★ ★

Traditional Creole desserts are often characterized by the presence of rum, pineapple, vanilla or banana. In this "Créolienne" our chef has used these traditional Creole elements and added the flavors of curry and oranges.

The classic ingredients in curry are coriander, cloves, cardamom, nutmeg and turmeric. Different varieties of curry emphasize some spices more than others. As Beaudelaire wrote, "spices, saphron powders, exotic dustings…lend elegance and appeal to any meal." The oranges need to marinate for at least twenty-four hours for the marmalade to turn out as desired. It should simmer until it reaches the consistency of purée. Grapefruit or pomelo can replace the orange, in which case the appropriate fruit would be used to decorate the cake.

The flavor of this cake depends greatly on the quality of the chocolate used. The particular method of melting the chocolate is not very important as long as the temperature is kept as low as possible during the process to ensure that the chocolate retains its glossiness when cool.

Few people can resist chocolate cake, and The "Créolienne" is sure to have many admirers.

1. Slice the orange, setting aside three pieces as a garnish. Dice the remainer, poach with the sugar and water for 15 minutes at a low simmer, and allow to cool. In a metal bowl, break up the chocolate and melt it together with the butter over a water bath. Use a wooden spoon to stir the chocolate.

2. Separate the eggs, reserving the whites. Add the egg yolks one by one to the chocolate, stirring constantly. Add the sugar and salt, and beat for about 5 minutes. Sift the flour over the chocolate and stir it in. In a separate bowl, whip the egg whites. Fold them into the chocolate.

"Créolienne"

3. Pour the chocolate batter into a buttered cake pan and bake for 30 minutes at 390 °F/200 °C. When the cake has cooled, slice it horizontally into 3 layers.

4. Whip the cream with the seeds of the vanilla bean and the curry. Place the first layer of cake on a serving dish and spread with orange marmalade. Cover with the second layer and spread it with whipped cream. Top with the last layer of cake, sprinkle with a little confectioners' sugar, and garnish with orange slices.

Tropical

For the sponge cake:
(see basic recipe)
6 eggs
¾ cup/180 g sugar
1½ cup plus 2 tsp/180 g flour
½ cup/60 g powdered cocoa

For the filling:
3 cups/750 ml whipping cream
⅓ cup/50 g confectioners' sugar
1 vanilla bean

½ cup plus 1 tbsp/50 g grated coconut
3 tbsp dark rum
1 passion fruit
1 banana
1 mango
1 small pineapple

For the garnish:
5¼ oz/150 g dark chocolate
a few pinches of grated coconut

Serves	*6*
Preparation time:	*35 minutes*
Cooking time:	*20 minutes*
Chilling time:	*1 hour*
Difficulty:	★ ★

That great classic of French baking tradition, the Black Forest Cake, gets its name from the famous German forest. Our chef has had the innovative idea of revising the original recipe and creating a Tropical Forest Cake

To go along with the tropical theme of the cake, our chef chose fruits such as banana, mango, passion fruit and pineapple. However, many variation will work as well. Guava will enhance the flavor of the mango, and zest of lime will add a pleasant tartness. Very juicy fruits, such as oranges or grapefruits, are not recommended in this recipe, as they would soak into the sponge cake and destroy the shape of the dessert.

Cream whips best when beaten with very cold utensils. Cooling the beater and bowl in advance will save time when making the whipped cream. Chocolate shavings and grated coconut make fitting garnish.

This cake must be eaten very fresh. For best results, it should be prepared the same day it is served, and should be refrigerated until serving to keep the cream cold.

1. To make the cake, break the eggs in a bowl and add the sugar. Beat with an electric mixer until tripled in volume.

2. Sift the flour and cocoa over the beaten eggs and sugar. Stir gently with a wooden spoon. Pour into a cake pan and bake for 20 minutes at 390 °F/200 °C. When the cake has cooled, slice it into 3 layers. Peel and dice the fruit for the filling and set aside.

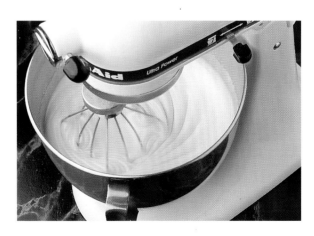

Forest Cake

3. Whip the cream and add the confectioners' sugar, the seeds of the vanilla bean and half the grated coconut. Carefully stir in 1 tbsp of the rum. Soak the bottom layer of the cake with 2 tsp rum.

4. Spread whipped cream on the first layer of cake, and sprinkle it with half the fruit and coconut. Repeat the process with the second layer after soaking it with 2 tsp of the rum. Top with the third layer soaked with 2 tsp rum, and spread with the remaining whipped cream. Cover the cake with chocolate shavings and sprinkle with grated coconut. Refrigerate for 1 hour before serving.

4 egg yolks
¾ cup plus 1 tbsp/200 g sugar
1 cup/250 g butter
2½ cups/300 g flour
a pinch of salt
¼ cup/30 g finely chopped almonds
⅓ cup/30 g grated coconut
4 tsp/20 ml rum
zest of 1 combava

For the garnish:
¼ cup/30 g powdered cocoa
1 egg
¼ cup/30 g confectioners' sugar

Serves	*6*
Preparation time:	*30 minutes*
Cooking time:	*45 minutes*
Difficulty:	★

In 1863 a native of Lorient presented the *Gâteau Breton* (Breton Cake) to the World Exposition. It is now known that it had its roots in the Caribbean, where it was traditionally prepared at home and taken to a communal oven to bake. It still has its place in family meals and religious gatherings in the Caribbean.

Our chef has adapted that classic recipe to pay homage to the many French sailors who sail the Caribbean seas.

This pirate's cake is very easy to prepare and keeps well. It can be stored by covering it in plastic wrap and keeping it in a dry place. It can also be frozen for up to several weeks.

The combava should be used sparingly because it is very strong and can overpower the other flavors, especially that of

the butter. The combava can be replaced by lime or lemon, as long as it is blanched first. The eggs and sugar should be well beaten until a smooth and homogenous liquid forms and it reaches the ribbon stage, i.e. the mixture will have a ribbon-like quality as it runs off the whisk or beaters. If these instructions are carefully followed, the Pirate's Special is guaranteed to have the perfect consistency.

Decorating this cake is very simple. Stencils cut out of paper and sprinkled with sugar or cocoa will do the trick.

1. Beat the eggs and sugar until a smooth, creamy mixture forms and it reaches the ribbon stage as described.

2. Soften the butter and beat into the egg mixture along with the flour, salt, almonds, grated coconut and rum.

Special

3. Stir in the combava zest.

4. Press the dough into a buttered mold or tart pan. Decorate the top of the pie with a fork if desired. Brush with beaten egg for color and bake at 285 °F/145 °C for 45 minutes. Cool and sprinkle with confectioners' sugar.

6 sheets of phyllo or *feuille de brick* pastry
8 bananas
⅓ cup/50 g finely chopped almonds
3½ tbsp/50 g brown sugar
3 pinches powdered or fresh sage
1 egg
butter to coat

Serves   4
Preparation time: 20 minutes
Cooking time: 20 minutes
Difficulty: ★

Packaged phyllo pastry is a great time-saver when making this sort of dessert. *Feuille de brick* pastry is similar to phyllo but far less readily available (see glossary for more information). It would be more authentic, but phyllo is an excellent substitute. When using phyllo pastry each sheet must be buttered to produce its characteristic crispiness when baked.

Our chef has chosen bananas for the filling and recommends using firm ones. However, other fruits can be used, as long as they are not too juicy. Guava or mango are good options. If juicy fruit such as oranges are used, the quantity of almonds should be increased to absorb some of the additional liquid.

Bread crumbs, though less flavorful than almonds, can also be used to absorb the excess liquid.

It is crucial for the pastry to be sealed, or it will fall apart when being unmolded and served. Brushing a beaten egg on the pastry will ensure a good seal between the layers.

Sage, which is well known for its medicinal uses, could be replaced by fresh or dried mint or even hyssop.

For individual servings, prepare this dessert in ramekins, using one sheet of phyllo pastry per serving. The pastry should be served on a plate with some vanilla or rum raisin ice cream.

1. In a large, high-sided, buttered baking pan, place the phyllo sheets so that they partially overlap. They should extend over the edges of the pan so that there is enough to fold back over the fruit. Add an extra layer of phyllo on the bottom to add strength to the pastry.

2. Peel the bananas, and cut them into thick slices. Gently stir in the almonds and brown sugar. Stir gently. Place half the bananas in the pan.

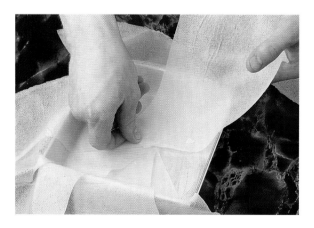

Pastry

3. Sprinkle with sage. Top with the remaining bananas and sprinkle with more sage.

4. Close the pastry by folding the leaves over the fruit, and use an egg to help seal it. Bake for 10 minutes at 390 °F/200 °C. Unmold the pastry, turn it over, and bake another 10 minutes until golden brown. Sprinkle with confectioners' sugar if desired, and serve warm.

Caribbean

½ cup/100 g candied orange peel
8 persimmons
⅓ cup/50 g raisins
⅓ cup/50 g white raisins
2 tbsp semolina
1 tsp walnut oil
3½ tbsp/50 g brown sugar

1 tsp cinnamon
8 tsp/20 g flour
3½ tbsp/50 ml dark rum
6½ tbsp/100 ml whipping cream

Short pastry: (see basic recipe)

Serves	6–8
Preparation time:	30 minutes
Resting time:	30 minutes
Cooking time:	40 minutes
Difficulty:	★

Quiche is a traditional dish of the Lorraine region, but its name is derived from the German word *kuchen*, which means "cake." Quiche has become a culinary classic. It is commonly made as a tart with cheese, ham, bacon, onion or other vegetables and served hot as an appetizer.

With this quiche our chef has designed a dessert with a similar appearance. He suggests starting it the night before it is to be served. To prevent the crust from shrinking, and to keep the edges from sinking, it should sit overnight or for a minimum of 30 minutes before baking.

The intense sweetness and pleasant flavor of the two varieties of raisins, combined with that of persimmon, will balance out the acidity of the orange peel. The semolina will absorb any excess liquid from the juicy pulp of the fruit as well as the walnut oil and prevent the pastry from becoming soggy. An extra teaspoon of semolina can be added if necessary.

Persimmon, cinnamon and rum form a trio of flavors outstanding both for their wonderful aroma and their beneficial effect on the digestion.

This quiche is an unusual dessert which is an excellent choice to round out a light meal.

1. Mince the candied orange peel. Peel and quarter the persimmons, then cut in thin slices.

2. Combine the persimmons, orange peel, both kinds of raisins, semolina and walnut oil.

Quiche

3. Make the short pastry and let it rest for at least 30 minutes. Roll it out on a floured surface, then ease it into a buttered (and preferably nonstick) 15 in/28–30 cm tart pan with high edges. In a bowl, combine the brown sugar, cinnamon and flour. Sprinkle this mixture over the pastry, then spoon the fruit mixture into it.

4. Lightly whip the cream, and gently blend in the rum. Spread the cream out over the fruit a spoonful at a time. Sprinkle with brown sugar. Bake for 40 minutes at 355 °F/180 °C. Let cool before unmolding and serve warm.

Pineapple Bread

For the dough:
1 tsp baker's yeast *
1⅔ cups/200 g flour
1 pinch of salt
1 pinch of lime zest
3½ tbsp/50 ml milk
1 egg
1 tbsp/15 g sugar
2 tbsp/30 g butter

For the pineapple pastry cream:
(see basic recipe)
1 pineapple
5 tbsp/75 g sugar

4 eggs
4 tsp cornstarch
8 tsp/20 g flour
1 tsp nutmeg
3½ tbsp/50 g butter

For the glaze:
3½ tbsp/50 g butter
3½ tbsp/50 g brown sugar
1 tbsp honey
confectioners' sugar (optional)

Serves	*4*
Preparation time:	*1 hour*
Chilling time:	*30 minutes*
Cooking time:	*25 minutes*
Difficulty:	★

With this creation, our chef honors one of the most famous islands of the Caribbean, St. Martin.

Ripe, juicy pineapple gives this bread a heavenly flavor. Once the butter has been added, the dough should be beaten until it no longer sticks to the sides of the bowl. This will signify that the dough has been mixed adequately.

The pastry cream can be varied by adding orange zest, or by replacing the nutmeg with vanilla. To lighten the pastry cream, our chef suggests pouring it through a strainer once it has been cooked. To prevent a skin from forming on its surface as it cools, a little butter can be spread over the pastry cream while it is still hot, which will form a protective barrier against the air. Pastry cream can be stored in the refrigerator in a sealed container for up to two days.

To fill the bread, sliced it lengthwise. Spread pastry cream on the bottom layer and then replace the top. Confectioners' sugar can be sprinkled on top if desired.

* In hot climates and tropical regions, substitute active dry yeast for the baker's yeast, halving the amount called for.

1. Crumble the yeast and stir it into the flour, salt and lime zest. Warm the milk and pout it into the flour mixture. Stir the ingredients until combined, then beat with an electric mixer for several minutes. Cover the bowl with a cloth and place it in a warm location to allow the mixture to rise for about 15-20 minutes.

2. Add the egg and sugar to the yeast dough and beat with an electric mixer. Prepare a pastry cream according to the basic recipe but substituting the ingredients listed above. Replace the milk with juice from the pineapple mixed with the nutmeg. Refrigerate for 30 minutes.

á la St.Martin

3. Beat the butter into the dough in small pieces. Continue beating until the dough no longer sticks to the sides of the bowl. Prepare the glaze: Melt the butter in a pan, stir in the sugar and honey until dissolved, then let cool.

4. Form the dough into a small, smooth ball and let it rest for 30 minutes on a lightly floured cookie sheet. Brush with the glaze. Bake at 355 °F/180 °C for 25 minutes. Once cooled, slice in half and fill with the pastry cream as described above.

Christopher

For the puff pastry:
(see basic recipe)
1¼ cups/150 g flour
a pinch of salt
2¾ cups/700 ml water
½ cup/120 g butter

Any seasonal fruit, for example:
1 mango
1 pomegranate
1 banana
1 orange
1 passion fruit
1 carambola (star fruit)
⅓ cup/100 g strawberries
1 papaya
1 kiwi
½ grapefruit
1 jar guava jelly

Serves	*8*
Preparation time:	*1 hour*
Cooking time:	*40 minutes*
Difficulty:	★ ★

How Christopher Columbus must have marvelled at the many varieties of fruit he discovered growing on the Caribbean islands! Our chef has tried to capture this feeling of discovery in this dazzling tart. The melange of fruit, blinding in its colors and flavors, piled in a delicious crust, will give the perfect touch to a pleasant meal and will surely be the triumph of the evening.

The passion fruit-flavored pastry cream, blended with whipped cream, is lighter and easier to digest than a traditional heavy pastry cream and a pleasant surprise for the palate.

Once the fruits are cut, they have a tendency to oxidize and darken. To prevent this, a little lemon juice can be squeezed over the fruit. Not only will the lemon save the appearance of the fruit, its tartness will also enhance the flavors of many of the other fruits, such as the banana.

If there are little "helpers" in the kitchen, they will enjoy braiding the lattice crust; it is just like playing with clay. In the interest of time, or to make it simpler, a clever shortcut can be used. Instead of braiding the strips of pastry, they can be laid on top of each other in a grid and gently flattened into each other. It is vital that the baking instructions be followed exactly: The pastry should be baked first at very high heat, then at low heat. This tart should be watched closely to prevent burning.

The lid serves only as decoration and the tart will work well without it, if time is short.

1. Prepare the passion fruit-flavored pastry cream as described in the basic recipe, but substituting the ingredients listed above. Whip the heavy cream, blend the liquers into it, and fold it into the pastry cream.

2. Prepare the puff pastry according the basic recipe using the ingredients listed above. Roll it out half of it and fit it into the tart pan. Prick it with a fork and prebake twice for 10 minutes at 390 °F/200 °C each time. Rub the crust with butter to protect it from the fruit juices. Spread the cream into the crust.

Columbus Tart

3. Make the lid by first rolling out strips of pastry about ⅜ in/1 cm wide. Lay them about ⅜ in/1 cm from each other. Braid in the others. Bake at 390 °F/200 °C for 10 minutes, then for 10 minutes at 340 °F/170 °C.

4. Decorate the pie with the sliced fruit, and brush the surface with warm guava jelly. Position the lid on the tart before serving.

Banana

For the almond-nut crust:
⅓ cup/50 g ground nuts
⅓ cup/50 g ground almonds
6½ tbsp/50 g confectioners' sugar
3 egg whites
6½ tbsp/100 g sugar

For the banana cream:
3 bananas
juice of 1 lemon
1 cup/250 ml milk
4 egg yolks
⅓ cup/40 g confectioners' sugar
2½ tbsp/20 g cornstarch
2 sheets of gelatin

8½ tbsp/130 g butter
1 cup/250 ml heavy cream

For the fruit filling:
1 small pineapple

For the Italian meringue:
2 egg whites
½ cup/125 g sugar
2 tbsp water

For the garnish:
seasonal fruit
apricot jam (optional)

Serves	*6*
Preparation time:	*1 hour*
Cooking time:	*20 minutes*
Chilling time:	*2 hours*
Difficulty:	★ ★

The crust of this pie is made of a variety of ground nuts. It can be replaced by a store-bought sponge cake layer. Grated coconut can also be used as a substitute for the nuts and will add an authentic tropical flavor.

The flavor of a banana develops as it ripens; fairly ripe bananas should therefore be chosen to give the cream the best possible taste. Overripe bananas should be avoided however because they will produce a floury consistency.

Adding lemon juice to the bananas will prevent them from blackening. However, no time should be wasted when making the cream and putting the pie together. Once the crust is prepared, add the banana cream immediately.

The meringue will be enhanced by adding a little color to it. A few drops of grenadine can be added when making the meringue, or the pie can be broiled for a few seconds to caramelize the top of the meringue. The garnishes should be placed on the pie after the broiling, of course!

A few, carefully arranged slices of whatever fruit is available will provide a suitable decoration. Brushing them with apricot jam will make them glisten and give even more visual appeal to this dessert. A sprig of fresh mint leaves will add the perfect dash of extra flavor and color.

1. Prepare the crust by sifting the nuts and almonds together, followed by the confectioners' sugar. Beat the egg whites until stiff, then beat in the sugar. Fold the whites into the dry ingredients with a slotted spoon. Spread the mixture on a lightly buttered and floured cookie sheet. Bake for 20 minutes at 355 °F/180 °C.

2. Prepare the banana cream: Slice the bananas and toss them in a bowl with the lemon juice. Beat the egg yolks and sugar together until they lighten in color. Stir in the cornstarch and bring to a boil. Remove from heat and add the gelatin, which should first be dissolved in a little water. Stir in the butter and the banana puree.

Cream Pie

3. Whip the cream and fold it into the slightly cooled banana mixture. Dice the pineapple. Make the meringue by beating the egg whites until stiff. Combine the water and sugar and heat it to 250 °F/120 °C. Pour it very slowly over the egg whites, beating continuously until cooled. Fit the crust into the desired mold, then cover it with the banana cream, filling the mold about halfway.

4. Sprinkle the pineapple over the banana cream. Place a second crust on the pineapple. Refrigerate for 2 hours. Remove the mold and cover the pie with the meringue. Decorate with fruit slices and apricot jelly.

1 small pineapple
1¼ cups/300 g sugar
2 cups/500 ml water
¼ cup/30 g confectioners' sugar
6 strawberries
1 lemon
2 tbsp dark rum

For the biscuit:
(see basic recipe)
4 eggs
¾ cup plus 1 tbsp/200 g sugar
1⅔ cups/200 g flour

For the Chiboust cream:
(see basic recipe)
1 cup/250 ml milk
1 egg
2 egg yolks
6½ tbsp/100 g sugar
½ cup/60 g flour
1 vanilla bean
⅔ cup/150 ml heavy cream
2 tbsp dark rum

Serves	8
Preparation time:	75 minutes
Cooking time:	35 minutes
Chilling time:	1 hour 45 minutes
Difficulty:	★

Traditionally, biscuit was baked twice, which is how it got its name: *bis* for twice and *cuit* for cooked. During the Crusades it was called *pain de pierre* or "rock bread," Chateaubriand, in his commentary on life in the New World, wrote: "always reduced to a solitary existence, I would eat a biscuit, a little sugar and lemon." Today, the method of baking it twice is no longer followed. The contemporary French *biscuit* is a sponge cake, similar to a genoise, but without any shortening, and therefore does not resemble the American roll-like biscuit at all.

Several different types of biscuit exist. The Savoy biscuit, the spoon biscuit and the Reims biscuit are all variations of the same idea. In this recipe, in which the quintessentially tropical flavors of rum and pineapple blend with the Chiboust cream,

our chef has created an exotic twist and named it after the beautiful island of St. Barthélemy in the Caribbean, also affectionately known as St. Barth's.

The Chiboust cream can be augmented with diced ripe mango. The addition of lemon juice to the glaze will keep it from being too cloyingly sweet. Because this cake will be inverted before serving, it is very important to take care with the arrangement of pineapple slices on the bottom of the baking pan, since they will become a garnish on the top of the desert when it is served.

Light, moist and tender, St. Barth's Biscuit will send your guests home dreaming of warm Carribean breezes.

1. Prepare the biscuit as described in the basic recipe but substituting the ingredients listed above. Once cooled, cut into 2 layers. Prepare the Chiboust cream according to the basic recipe, but using the ingredients listed above. Refrigerate for 45 minutes. Peel and slice the pineapple, being careful to remove all the small black "eyes."

2. Poach the pineapple slices in the water and sugar and let simmer for 30 minutes. Drain and lightly sauté them in a pan with the confectioners' sugar. To make the glaze, reduce half the liquid for 5 minutes, then add 3 strawberries and the juice of half a lemon.

Biscuit

3. Line a baking pan with the sautéed pineapple slices. Add the rum to the glaze. Place the first biscuit layer, soaked in a little of the glaze, on the pineapple slices.

4. Pour in the Chiboust cream and cover it with the second layer of biscuit, also soaked in glaze. Place a weight on top of the pan and refrigerate for 1 hour. Unmold the cake and decorate with additional glaze and strawberries.

For the puff pastry:
(see basic recipe)
2½ cups/300 g flour
⅔ cup/80 g powdered cocoa
⅔ cup/150 ml water
¾ cup plus 3 tbsp/220 g butter
1 pinch of salt

For the filling:
7 oz/200 g white chocolate
¾ cup/200 ml heavy cream

1¼ cups/150 g confectioners' sugar
3½ tbsp/50 ml white rum
1 cup/150 g candied citron

For the garnish:
confectioners' sugar
powdered cocoa

Serves	8
Preparation time:	2 hours
Cooking time:	25 minutes
Chilling time:	90 minutes
Difficulty:	★ ★ ★

Citron has been cultivated since the third century BC. Citron resembles lemon, which belongs to the same family, but the citron is larger, its skin is much thicker, and its pulp is much less juicy. It is principally used for its rind and to make jams and marmalades. It can also be used to make a liqueur. The citron tree is particularly aromatic, from its roots to its leaves. In the Jewish religion, the citron or *etrog*, plays a key role during the autumn holiday of Sukkot, the Feast of Tabernacles, in which a perfect citron is shaken in all directions along with a bouquet of myrtle, willow and palm.

Our chef has chosen the citron because its rind, once candied, will lend its flavor to the pastry. The directions for preparing the pastry are unusual and should be followed carefully. Each rectangle should be placed on a cookie sheet, covered with a piece of wax paper, and flattened by another cookie sheet while baking. This prevents the pastry from rising or warping and preserves its light and delicate texture.

The checkerboard is made by cutting out strips of paper approximately 1 in/2 cm wide and forming a lattice on the pastry. A checkerboard pattern is formed by sprinkling confectioners' sugar over the paper. The strips should be removed very carefully and placed over the sugar; then powdered cocoa is sprinkled on the pastry to make the brown squares.

1. Prepare a puff pastry as described in the basic recipes, but substituting the ingredients listed above. Adjust the basic recipe so that the flour and cocoa are combined.

2. When the pastry has rested for two 20-minute periods, fold it in thirds one last time and let it rest a final 20 minutes.

Checkerboard

3. Prepare the white chocolate filling by melting the white chocolate in a double boiler. In a separate bowl, whipped the cream. Fold the whipped cream along with the confectioners' sugar into the melted and cooled chocolate. Pour in the rum. Chop the citron and blend it in as well.

4. Cut 2 rectangles measuring 10x16 in/25x40 cm and bake for 20 minutes at 390 °F/200 °C. Once cooled, cut them in rectangles measuring 4x10 in/10x25 cm. Assemble the pastry by layering the pastry rectangles with the cream filling, beginning and ending with pastry. Decorate and refrigerate for 1½ hours before serving.

The Caribbean

7 oz/200 g lady fingers
3 tbsp/20 g pistachios (optional)

For the sponge cake:
  (see basic recipe)
3 egg yolks
6½ tbsp/100 g sugar
¾ cup plus 1 tbsp/100 g flour
2 pinches of nutmeg

For the syrup:
6½ tbsp/100 ml water
3½ tbsp/50 g sugar
6½ tbsp/100 ml orange-flavored liqueur

For the filling:
1 lb/500 g papaya
2½ tbsp/50 g papaya jelly

For the custard:
  (see basic recipe)
1 cup/250 ml milk
3½ tbsp/50 g sugar
3 egg yolks
3 sheets of gelatin
2 pinches of nutmeg
½ cup water
¾ cup/200 ml whipping cream

Serves	8
Preparation time:	2 hours
Cooking time:	23 minutes
Chilling time:	2 hours
Difficulty:	★ ★

The sponge layer of this dessert requires deft handling. Our chef suggests the flour and nutmeg be sifted together before adding to the fragile egg and sugar mixture. This will reduce the time necessary to blend the the ingredients with the egg, and prevent the sponge from collapsing from overbeating. A packet of yeast can be added as additional insurance against a fallen sponge. A no-fail method, of course, is to buy the sponge cake at the store!

It is important that the ladyfingers do not absorb too much liquid or they will disintegrate. The custard should be completely cooled before it is combined with the whipped cream. Otherwise, the cream may melt and weigh down the custard rather than lighten it. Our chef suggests constructing the cake "upside down." After the ladyfingers are in place, the papaya slices should be laid on the bottom of the pan. Pour about one fourth of the custard over them. It should then be refrigerated for 10 minutes. The next step is to cover the custard with a layer of sponge cake. Another layer of fruit, the second piece of sponge cake and the Caribbean Diplomat is done! The cake should be refrigerated for two hours before being served.

A handy trick for unmolding this sort of dessert is to soak the mold in warm water, or run the bottom under the faucet. This will loosen the ladyfingers from the edges. The final step is to brush on papaya jelly to give the cake a good glaze and then add a few pistachios for color.

1. For the sponge cake, beat the egg yolks and sugar in a double boiler until they reach the ribbon stage (about 5 minutes). Combine the flour and nutmeg, then sift into the egg yolks.

2. Butter and flour a mold. Invert the mold and tap it to remove the excess flour. Fill the mold with the batter and bake for 15 minutes at 390 °F/200 °C. Unmold. Cool and slice into 2 layers.

Diplomat

3. Prepare the syrup with water, sugar and the orange-flavored liqueur. Let boil for 3 minutes. Slice the ladyfingers in half lengthwise and moisten them in the syrup. Stand them up against the sides of the mold cut edge up. Peel, seed and slice the papaya and lay the slices on the bottom of the pan. Reserve extra slices.

4. Prepare the custard as described in the basic recipes but substituting the ingredients listed above. Combine the nutmeg with the gelatin and water. Cover the papayas with one fourth of the custard. Whip the cream and fold it into the remaining cooled custard. Assemble the cake as described in the text and chill for 2 hours before serving.

Grapefruit and

For the topping:
1 pink grapefruit
1 pomegranate
6½ tbsp/100 g sugar
3½ tbsp/50 g brown sugar
1½ cups water
3½ tbsp/50 ml grenadine

For the short pastry:
(see basic recipe)
1⅔ cups/200 g flour
6½ tbsp/100 g butter
1 egg
2 tbsp water
2½ tbsp/40 g sugar
1 pinch of salt

For the grapefruit cream:
1 tsp cornstarch
juice of 1 pink grapefruit
2 eggs
1 egg yolk
6½ tbsp/100 g sugar
¾ cup white rum
5 tbsp/75 g butter

Serves	*6*
Preparation time:	*45 minutes*
Cooking time:	*1 hour 5 minutes*
Chilling time:	*1 hour 30 minutes*
Difficulty:	★ ★

The pomegranate is traditionally served during the Jewish New Year, which occurs in early autumn. It is used as a centerpiece because, as one legend goes, it has 613 seeds representing the 613 commandments. In the Far East, pomegranate is a symbol of love and fertility because of its color and the abundance of its seeds. The fruit is also used as a dye in many prized Middle Eastern rugs.

Because of the intense color of the juice, the seeds must be added at the right time so they do not leave brownish-red blotches in the cream.

The novelty of this dessert, in both its shape and flavor, lies in the combination of pomegranate and grapefruit. To help the grapefruits maintain their pink color, a little grenadine can be added while they are being candied.

Once the grapefruit is peeled and sliced, it becomes very fragile. A large spatula is a good utensil to handle the slices without breaking them.

For an added crunch, this tart can be sprinkled with confectioners' sugar and then broiled for a few minutes, creating a thin layer of caramel on the top. One precaution: The pastry burns easily and should therefore be closely watched while under the broiler.

1. Peel the grapefruit for the topping with a very sharp knife. Slice thinly and remove any seeds. Cut the pomegranate into quarters and scoop out the seeds, being careful to remove any bits of the white membrane. Prepare the short pastry, let it rest 30 minutes, then roll it out and fit it into a tart pan. Prebake it twice, for 10 minutes each time at 390 °F/200 °C. Set aside.

2. To candy the grapefruit, place the slices in a pan and sprinkle them with the sugars. Add the water and grenadine. Lightly simmer for 40 minutes. Remove from heat and let the slices cool on a plate for 25 to 30 minutes. Save the candied juice.

Pomegranate Tart

3. To prepare the grapefruit cream, dissolve the cornstarch in a bowl with the grapefruit juice. In a separate bowl, combine the eggs, egg yolks, sugar, rum and then the dissolved cornstarch. Bring this to a boil, stirring constantly. Remove from heat and beat in the butter, piece by piece.

4. Spread the grapefruit cream on the bottom of the tart. Lay the candied grapefruit on the cream, surrounded by the pomegranate seeds. Reduce the candied juice to create a glaze, stirring in some gelatin if necessary. Glaze the tart and refrigerate for 1½ hours.

Granny Aline's

4 guavas
6½ tbsp/100 g brown sugar
8¾ oz/250 g gingerbread
6 sheets of gelatin
2 cups/500 ml heavy cream

For the custard:
 (see basic recipe)
8 egg yolks
4 cups/1 liter milk
2½ cups/600 g sugar
2 vanilla beans

For the cinnamon shortbread:
 (see basic recipe)
2 cups/250 g flour
1 cup/125 g finely ground almonds
½ cup/125 g brown sugar
2 eggs
¾ cup/170 g butter
a pinch of salt
a pinch of cinnamon

Serves	6
Preparation time:	40 minutes
Cooking time:	20 minutes
Chilling time:	1 hour 25 minutes
Difficulty:	★ ★

Our chef was inspired to create this dessert by his Granny Aline, who took care of him when he was a child. Raised by her in his parent's home, he quickly grew fond of the exotic flavors in her desserts such as passion fruit, papaya or guava.

Guava pulp is very soft and melts in the mouth. While the tartness varies from species to species, it is generally reminiscent of peach and quince. Gauva is most commonly used in guava jelly and guava juice. A guava puree would be a flavorful addition to the dessert.

After quartering the guava, it must be sprinkled heavily with sugar—brown sugar is preferable—to draw the juice from it. It will thus become candied without being cooked. The layer of shortbread will support the cake.

A small amount of diced guava can be added to the cream itself, to create a more intense guava flavor. A little liqueur can be added to the gingerbread to give this distinctive cake even more personality. Our chef has a further excellent suggestion for unmolding the cake with ease: If the mold is lined with wax paper, the cake can easily be removed from the mold. Carefully peel the wax paper from the cake before serving.

This fruit dessert will make an unforgettable finish for any gathering, perhaps even for a family reunion.

1. Peel and quarter the guava. Place the slices in a bowl and sprinkle them with the brown sugar.

2. Soak the gingerbread in milk and then prepare the custard according to the directions in the basic recipe but substituting the ingredients listed above. Dissolve the gelatin in water and stir it into the custard. Whip the cream and fold it into the cooled custard. Blend very gently.

Upside-Down Cake

3. Prepare the shortbread pastry as described in the basic recipes but substituting the ingredients listed above. Let rest 20 minutes. Roll out the pastry and cut out a circle the same size as the largest part of the mold. Bake for 20 minutes at 355 °F/200 °C, then let cool.

4. Arrange the guava slices on the bottom of the mold. Pour in custard to fill the mold halfway. Cover with gingerbread and pour the remaining custard over it. Refrigerate for 1 hour. Unmold the cake onto the shortbread disk and serve immediately.

3 persimmons
4½ tbsp/70 g sugar
3½ tbsp/50 ml litchi liqueur
4 sheets of gelatin
⅔ cup/150 ml heavy cream
6½ tbsp/100 g butter

For the vanilla custard:
  (see basic recipe)
1 cup/250 ml milk
3 egg yolks
8 tsp/40 g sugar
1 vanilla bean

For the sponge cake:
  (see basic recipe)
2 egg yolks
¼ cup/60 g sugar
½ cup/60 g flour

For the garnish:
1 persimmon
1½ tbsp/30 g guava jelly (optional)

Serves | 6
Preparation time: | 50 minutes
Cooking time: | 25 minutes
Chilling time: | 1 hour 40 minutes
Difficulty: | ★ ★

Carmel Cake is very similar to the Caribbean Diplomat Cake, also included in this book. The custard gives it the appearance of a flan or pudding.

This cake originated in a convent in Haifa but owes its exotic taste to our chef, who added persimmons to the recipe. Persimmons are a very popular fruit in this area.

The firm consistency of the persimmon is perfect for baking. It can, however, be replaced by papaya or apple. If the persimmons have not quite reached full ripeness, they should be baked for 15 minutes at 300 °F/150 °C instead of being macerated in the sugar and liqueur. This will tenderize them and make them less sweet.

To create this lovely dessert when there is not much time, a store-bought sponge layer may be used. If litchi liqueur is unavailable, it can easily be replaced byTriple Sec or dark rum.

Reserve several slices of fruit to garnish the top of the cake. It can then be brushed with warm guava jelly for a picture-perfect presentation.

1. Slice the persimmons and allow them to macerate in the sugar and litchi liqueur.

2. Prepare a custard according to the basic recipe but substituting the ingredients listed above. Dissolve the gelatin in some water and then stir it into the custard. Whip the cream and fold it in as well. Prepare a sponge cake according to the basic recipe but substituting the ingredients listed above. Bake at 340 °F/170 °C for 20 minutes.

Cake

3. Slice the sponge cake and lightly sauté it in the butter. Line the sides and bottom of the mold with the cake. Place a layer of persimmon slices on the cake, and pour in enough custard to cover them. Refrigerate for 10 minutes.

4. Pour in the remaining custard, and refrigerate 1½ hours. Unmold the cake by setting the mold in warm water which will help loosen the cake from the edges of the pan. Garnish with a few slices of persimmon and brush with warm guava jelly.

Josephine's

1 lb/500 g pink grapefruit

For the marzipan:
  (see basic recipe)
1¼ cups/300 g sugar
2 cups/250 g finely chopped almonds
3 egg whites
orange zest
1 tbsp orange-flower water

For the grapefruit coulis:
1 grapefruit
4½ tbsp/100 g guava jelly
3½ tbsp/50 ml white rum
1 pinch nutmeg

For the royal icing:
1 egg white
juice of 1 lime
1¼ cups/150 g confectioners' sugar

Serves	6
Preparation time:	35 minutes
Cooking time:	33 minutes
Difficulty:	★

Honoré de Balzac immortalized the town of Issoudun in 1844. The flyer that was circulated to announce that the novelist was opening a store in Paris to sell marzipan from Issoudun told of "this sweet, one of the greatest creations in the history of sweets, whose reputation was made 1,000 years ago..."

This beautiful dessert unites many of the flavors of the Caribbean, and retains an exotic taste while still allowing for variation, since the fruits recommended here can be replaced by others. Pomelo or mandarin oranges are two delicious possibilities, for example.

The torte can be prepared several days in advance and freezes well. However, it should not be refrigerated after it has been iced, as this will cause it to become soggy. The torte can also be made in ramekins for individual servings.

The guava-grapefruit coulis is a marvelous accompaniment, but if other fruits are substituted for the topping, they should be used in the coulis as well. The nutmeg should not be replaced because it suits any fruit well.

The many flavors of this torte will surely intrigue and delight your guests.

1. Prepare the marzipan as described in the basic recipes but substituting the ingredients listed above. Be sure to add the orange zest and the orange-blossom water. Prepare a coulis by puréeing the grapefruit and guava jelly. Add them to the rum and the nutmeg, then refrigerate.

2. Press the marzipan into a buttered pie pan and bake it for 30 minutes at 355 °F/280 °C. Let cool.

Marzipan Torte

3. Prepare the royal icing (see basic recipe for marzipan). Whip the egg white, lime juice, and confectioners' sugar together. Spread out over the marzipan and bake at 430 °F/ 220 °C for 3 minutes to harden.

4. Slice the grapefruit in quarters, removing all the skin. Garnish the torte with grapefruit peel, wrapped in the shape of a flower, and some slices of grapefruit. Add some red currents or a leaf from your garden if desired.

Sponge cake (see basic recipe)

For the fruit salad:
1 banana
1 mango
1 papaya
1 apricot
2 kiwis
1 apple
1 lemon
½ small pineapple
½ cup/100 g pitted prunes
⅓ cup/50 g white raisins
2 tbsp passion fruit liqueur

For the mousse:
6½ tbsp/100 ml milk
2 egg yolks
2 tsp/10 g sugar
4 tsp/10 g cornstarch
½ vanilla bean
3 ½ tbsp/50 g butter

For the Italian meringue:
3 egg whites
½ cup plus 2 tbsp/150 g sugar
4 tbsp apricot jam
¾ cup/200 ml sugar syrup (see basic recipe)

Serves	8
Preparation time:	2 hours 30 minutes
Cooking time:	20 minutes
Chilling time:	2 hours
Difficulty:	★ ★ ★

During a trip to Martinique our chef was struck by the beauty of Mt. Pelé, an extinct volcano on this "Island of the Beautiful Flowers." He wanted to pay homage to the mountain by creating a dessert that would require great effort and skill and which would impress the most demanding of guests.

Purchasing a sponge cake at the grocery will allow more time to be spent on the rest of the preparation, and will not affect the quality. The diced fruit should be very firm and sprinkled first with lemon juice to prevent oxidization, then with the passion fruit liqueur. The prunes should be coarsely chopped and added along with the raisins. Once this is done, the fruit should be drained. Reserve the most flawless pieces of fruit for the garnish.

The next step is to prepare the sponge cake. It should be cut into two layers with a serrated knife, and the top layer should be set aside. The instructions for pastry cream in the basic recipes should be followed in preparing the mousse. However, the softened butter should be added to the warm cream and beaten until the cream has completely cooled. Some passion fruit liqueur will improve its flavor. For the meringue, the eggs and sugar should be beaten in a metal bowl over a water bath. When the mixture reaches 95 °F/ 35 °C it should be removed from the heat and beaten until it cools completely. If a stationary mixer is available, the water bath can be eliminated, and a blow torch used to heat the outside of the bowl.

1. Prepare the sponge cake (see basic recipe). Butter and flour a baking pan and bake the cake for 20 minutes at 340 °F/170 °C. Peel and cube the fruits, and macerate them in the passion fruit liqueur. Strain them and reserve the liquid.

2. Prepare the mousse as explained above and fold in the fruit. Unmold the sponge cake. To slice the cake, insert the knife at an angle so that you carve out a convex slice. This will create a "bowl" in which to place the mousse. The top layer will create a dome.

Pelé

3. Lightly sprinkle both the cake layers with the marinade. Place the fruit mousse in the "bowl" of the sponge cake. Set the second, convex disk of sponge on the mousse to create a dome.

4. Prepare the Italian meringue as described above. Cover the dome with the meringue using a spatula or a pastry bag. Broil it for a few seconds to brown lightly. Decorate the top of the cake with a few slices of fruit. Refrigerate for 2 hours before serving.

Papaya

1 lb/500 g papaya
3½ tbsp/50 g butter
⅓ cup/80 g sugar

For the crêpe batter:
1⅔ cups/400 ml milk
3 eggs
3½ tbsp/50 g sugar
1 tsp powdered ginger
1 cup/125 g flour
½ cup/125 g butter
2 egg whites

For the papaya chutney:
1 lb/500 g papaya
2 cups/500 g sugar
juice of 1 lime
zest of one orange
4 tsp pepper

Serves	6
Preparation time:	40 minutes
Cooking time:	30 minutes
Chilling time:	3 hours
Difficulty:	★

Papaya skin, which is very thin and should always be removed, is a good indicator of the fruit's ripeness. It will change from green to yellow as it ripens. Green papaya can be eaten as a vegetable in a gratin, in a puree or even fried. Once it turns yellow, it can be eaten in slices like a melon, in a fruit salad or made into jam.

To decorate the cake, our chef recommends yellow papayas which are still firm. They should be briefly seared over high heat to prevent them from turning into jam.

The egg whites, which are beaten and added to the crêpe batter, contribute to the lightness of the cake. The batter should be baked briefly before adding the papaya to allow the fruit to spread out evenly instead of clumping at the bottom.

The papaya chutney which accompanies this cake can be made two different ways. It should either be delicately stirred as it cooks to preserve the shape of the fruit, or it can be cooked until it reaches an almost jam like consistency.

Papaya is a particularly mild fruit and lemon or lime is often used to help bring out its flavor. For an interesting twist, orange or even a little vinegar may be used. Papaya chutney, with a little pepper or vinegar, is also an excellent accompaniment to most game dishes.

1. To prepare the crêpe batter, combine the milk, eggs, sugar and ginger. Sift the flour into the mixture. Melt the butter and stir it in. Fold in the the beaten egg whites. Let this rest for 30 minutes.

2. Peel and slice the papayas. Sauté them over high heat for 5 minutes in the butter and the sugar.

Ring

3. Pour the crêpe batter in a buttered bundt pan. Bake for 5 minutes at 220 °F/430 °C. Remove the pan from the oven. Quickly add the papaya slices and bake again for 20 minutes at 355 °F/180 °C. Refrigerate for 2 hours.

4. To make the papaya chutney, dice the papayas and combine with the sugar, lime juice, minced orange zest and pepper. Cook over medium heat for 30 minutes until the fruits are candied. Refrigerate 1 hour before serving.

½ cup plus 1 tbsp/200 g coconut jam
1 pineapple
3½ tbsp/50 ml dark rum
6½ tbsp/100 g sugar

For the short pastry:
   (see basic recipe)
2 cups/250 g flour
½ cup/125 g butter
1 egg
5 tsp water
1 vanilla bean
a pinch of salt

For the pastry cream:
   (see basic recipe)
2 cups/500 ml milk
1 vanilla bean
½ cup/125 g sugar
3½ tbsp/25 g flour
3 egg yolks

For the garnish:
6½ tbsp/50 g confectioners' sugar
a few candied kumquats

Serves	*8*
Preparation time:	*2 hours 30 minutes*
Cooking time:	*1 hour 30 minutes*
Chilling time:	*2 hours*
Difficulty:	★ ★

The *Tourment d'Amour* ("torment of love") is a very traditional cake from the town of Les Saintes in Guadeloupe. This cake evokes all the romance of the two islands of Guadeloupe: Terre de Haut and Terre de Bas. On a more practical note, it is also deliciously moist and flavorful.

Our chef has created an updated *Tourment d'Amour* cake by combining rum with pineapple. He departs from the traditional recipe by using candied pineapple, which accentuates its exotic flavor in this cake. The combination of the coconut and rum is reminiscent of a classic and refreshing piña colada. A very ripe pineapple is best suited for this recipe. It should be cooked until completely dry or until it begins to caramelize.

This is the perfect cake for a birthday or other special occasion when an inscription on the cake is desired. Simply melt a little chocolate in a double boiler and then place it in a cone of wax paper with the tip cut off to write on the cake. If the chocolate hardens too quickly, just place the cone in the microwave for a few seconds. The cake should be closely monitored as it bakes. When the color is just right, a sheet of wax paper should be placed over the cake to keep it from burning. Cococnut can be sprinkled on top of the cake rather than confectioners' sugar, and the whole cake will be livened up with a few slices of candied kumquat.

This is the perfect dessert for an intimate dinner.

1. Prepare the short pastry as described in the basic recipe but substituting the ingredients listed above. Roll it out and fit it into a highsided pan with a removable bottom (such as a springform pan). Prick the pastry with a fork and bake for 5 minutes. Spread the coconut jam on the bottom.

2. Dice the pineapple, and combine it with the rum and sugar. Cook until it begins to caramelize.

Torment

3. Fill the crust with the candied pineapple. Prepare a pastry cream as described in the basic recipe but substituting the ingredients listed above. Cook it for 5 minutes.

4. Fill the crust with the pastry cream. Bake for 15 minutes at 390 °F/ 200 °C then for 25 minutes at 340 °F/170 °C. Once cooled, refrigerate for 2 hours. Sprinkle with confectioners' sugar or decorate with your choice of toppings (chocolate, candied fruit...).

For the coconut pastry:
4 egg whites
2¼ cups/200 g grated coconut
6½ tbsp/100 g sugar
zest of 1 lemon
a pinch of cinnamon

For the shortbread:
  (see basic recipe)
1¼ cups/150 g flour
5 tbsp/75 g butter
a pinch of salt
water

For the chutney:
1 mango
½ pineapple
1 small guava
1 kiwi
1 passion fruit
1 banana
⅓ cup/50 g raisins
pinch of pepper
1 tsp grated ginger
a pinch of *poudre de colombo*
juice of 1 lemon

Serves	*6*
Preparation time:	*1 hour*
Cooking time:	*2 hours 55 minutes*
Chilling time:	*1 hour*
Difficulty:	★ ★

These "rocks" are a traditional form of pastry which typically have an irregular shape and a bumpy, rocky texture. There are many variations, for example the dough is often prepared with almonds or coconut, or with chocolate and raisins, as in the well-known Congolais. These pastries are a favorite treat often served with tea.

The chutney used here has been derived from the famous English chutney made by deglazing caramel with vinegar and then cooking it slowly until it develops its characteristic taste.

The coconut pastry will keep well if it is properly sealed and refrigerated. Dried coconut works better than fresh coconut since it contains less moisture. The egg whites can be beaten before being added to the coconut mixture. Adding a little lemon juice helps the egg whites stiffen (one teaspoon for two or three egg whites).

This simple recipe is real treat for coconut lovers and for children. It should be served warm with a good champagne after a meal or with tea for a snack.

1. Prepare the coconut pastry by beating the egg whites in a bowl containing the grated coconut, sugar, lemon zest and a pinch of cinnamon. This will be the "rock" pastry.

2. Prepare the shortbread following the instructions in the basic recipe but substituting the ingredients listed above. Let it rest for 20 minutes, then roll it out into an oval and prick with a fork. Place the "rock" pastry in a pastry bag and form a ring around the edge of the shortbread. Make several additional little "rocks" directly on a cookie sheet. Bake at 390 °F/200 °C for 25 minutes.

Coconut Island

3. To make the chutney, peel and dice all the fruit. In a large pan, cook the fruit, raisins, pepper, colombo powder and grated ginger in the lemon juice. Simmer lightly for 2–2½ hours until it caramelizes.

4. Fill the crust with the chutney and then top with the "rocks." Refrigerate for 1 hour before serving.

Lemon-Lime

For the filling:
1 lemon
1 lime
1 passion fruit
1⅔ cups/400 ml water
4 egg yolks
½ cup plus 2 tbsp/150 g sugar
⅓ cup/40 g cornstarch
2 tbsp/30 g butter
3½ tbsp/50 ml dark rum

For the shortbread:
  (see basic recipe)
1⅔ cups/200 g flour
6½ tbsp/100 g butter
3½ tbsp/50 g sugar
1 egg
a pinch of salt

For the meringue:
3 egg whites
a pinch of salt
½ cup plus 2 tbsp/150 g sugar
6½ tbsp/100 ml water

Serves	*6*
Preparation time:	*1 hour*
Cooking time:	*45 minutes*
Difficulty:	★ ★

Meringue has many different forms and consistencies. Whether one likes it crunchy, light or sticky, all the credit is due to a Swiss pastry chef from the town of Meiringen who invented meringue in 1720, according to legend.

In this recipe, the meringue is made Italian style since the sugar is cooked before being beaten into the eggs. However, it can just as easily be made in the so-called French style, i.e. without cooking the sugar.

The Italian style does have the advantage of keeping a little longer if this dessert is prepared in advance. The French method however, is less time consuming since one step is omitted. When preparing an Italian meringue, watch the bubbles: When large ones resembling blisters form, the sugar syrup is done.

The pie can be broiled a few seconds if it has not browned enough, but care must be taken to prevent burning the meringue. If there is leftover egg white, it can used to make meringue kisses. Shapes can be formed with a pastry bag and various tips, and baked for about one hour at 175 °F/180 °C. The combination of lime juice, lemon juice and passion fruit will add a heavenly flavor to the egg whites as they bake.

1. Remove the zest from the lemon and lime. Juice the lime and lemon, and combine with the water. Remove the pulp from the passion fruit and boil it in the lemon-lime juice. Let the passion fruit steep in the liquid, then remove it. Prepare the shortbread as described in the basic recipe but substituting the ingredients listed above. Let it rest for 30 minutes.

2. Beat the egg yolks and sugar until light, then add the cornstarch. Pour in the boiling lemon-lime juice. Bring this mixture to a boil while continuously stirring. Remove from heat and add the butter, rum and lemon and lime zest.

Passion Meringue

3. Roll out the shortbread. Fit it into a tart pan and bake it twice for 10 minutes each time at 390 °F/200 °C. Once cooled, fill it halfway with the citrus cream.

4. For the meringue, first boil the sugar and water at 250 °F/120 °C for 5 minutes. Beat the egg whites with a pinch of salt. Pour the hot sugar syrup over the egg whites and continue beating until completely cooled. Using a pastry bag, cover the pie with meringue. Bake at 355 °F/180 °C for 20 minutes.

Afro-Caribbean

For the puff pastry:
(see basic recipe)
2½ cups/300 g flour
½ cup/60 g cocoa powder
⅔ cup/150 ml water
¾ cup plus 3 tbsp/225 g butter
a pinch of salt

For the hazelnut caramel:
4 tbsp water
½ cup plus 2 tbsp/150 g sugar
¾ cup/100 g hazelnuts

For the filling:
8¾ oz/250 g bitter chocolate
1¼ cups/300 ml heavy cream
½ cup/100 g candied orange peel
8 tsp/20 g confectioners' sugar

Serves	*6*
Preparation time:	*1 hour 30 minutes*
Cooking time:	*35 minutes*
Chilling time:	*1 hour*
Difficulty:	★ ★ ★

Just the thought of making puff pastry is often discouraging since the directions seem complicated and difficult. This is truly not the case! Making a good puff pastry is only a question of coordination and common sense. The most important step is making sure the butter is evenly distributed and does not form lumps in the pastry. This is what gives the pastry its "puff." Of course, store-bought puff pastry is even easier and does save considerable time.

Our chef notes that it is important to prevent the pastry from rising as it bakes. To do so, it should be weighed down with a cookie sheet. A layer of wax paper will keep the pastry from sticking to the extra cookie sheet and also keep it clean.

The carmelization of the hazelnuts is a delicate operation. The sugar should cook at 275 °F/140 °C. As soon as it begins to caramelize, the hazelnuts should be stirred in and the caramel removed from the heat to prevent the sugar from burning and becoming bitter.

The construction of the millefeuille is repetitive. The first layer of pastry should be covered in puffs of cream with the help of a pastry bag. Extra cream should be added in the middle and one-third of the hazelnut/orange mixture should be spooned on the cream. Repeat for the second and third layers.

There you have it! The millefeuille can be garnished by adding orange slices or a molded chocolate rose.

1. Prepare the puff pastry as described in the basic recipe but using the ingredients above. Sift the cocoa and flour together before adding to the pastry. Roll it out into 3 identical layers and prick them with a fork. Bake for 20 minutes at 390 °F/200 °C between 2 cookie sheets, being sure to protect the top of the pastry with a sheet of wax paper. Once baked, sprinkle with confectioners' sugar while still hot.

2. For the caramel, combine the sugar and water in a heavy-bottomed pan and bring to a boil. As soon as it begins to brown, add the hazelnuts. Stir until a caramel forms around the hazelnuts. Spread this out on an oiled cookie sheet or other flat surface and let cool.

Millefeuille

3. For the filling, melt the chocolate in a double boiler. Whip the cream, then fold it into the cooled chocolate. Keep at room temperature.

4. Coarsely grind the caramelized nuts and combine them with the candied orange peel. Put the millefeuille together as described in the text and decorate it. Refrigerate for 1 hour before serving.

Pomelo Crêpe

For the crêpe batter:
  (see basic recipe)
1¼ cups/150 g flour
2 large eggs
2 tbsp sugar
a pinch of salt
zest of 1 lime
1¼ cups/300 ml milk

For the pomelo cream:
3 eggs
¾ cup plus 1 tbsp/200 g sugar
¾ cup/200 ml pomelo juice
6½ tbsp/50 g flour
5 tbsp/75 g butter
2 sheets of gelatin

confectiioners' sugar for glaze

Serves	*6*
Preparation time:	*25 minutes*
Cooking time:	*30 minutes*
Chilling time:	*45 minutes*
Difficulty:	★

Traditionally crêpes were only made during Carnival and Mardi Gras, but today they are popular during all seasons and holidays. There are three signs of a good crêpe: its fluffiness, its crispness and its doneness. To give crêpes an even lighter consistency, some beer or watered-down milk can be added to the batter. Crêpes made without sugar will remain stiff when stacked. If sugar is used in the batter, it will melt and make the crêpes soggy. If melted butter is added to the batter, it is not necessary to grease the pan.

In this recipe, our chef has suggested making slightly thicker crêpes, which will guarantee a better shape for the millefeuille.

For the final garnish, a thin piece of metal should be heated over a flame until red and lightly placed on the confectioners' sugar in a lattice pattern. A kabob skewer will do the trick. But care should be taken to avoid being burned!

A personal touch can be added to the decoration of this dessert by changing the designs on the top of the millefeuille. Other possible variations include substituting the pomelo with grapefruit or oranges.

This surprising dessert is sure to become a favorite, especially for a snack or a birthday.

1. In a metal bowl, combine the flour, eggs, sugar, salt, lime zest and milk with a whisk. Let the batter rest 30 minutes. Lightly butter a frying pan over low heat. Pour a ladleful of batter in the pan. Flip the crêpe when it turns golden brown. Repeat until all the batter has been used.

2. Make the pomelo cream by mixing the eggs, sugar, pomelo juice and flour. Stir over low heat until the mixture thickens.

Millefeuille

3. Slice the butter and stir into the pomelo cream. Bring to a boil. Melt the gelatin in a little cold water. Pour the pomelo cream into a metal mixing bowl and stir in the dissolved gelatin.

4. Form the millefeuille directly on the serving dish. Using the ring from a springform pan to hold it steady, alternately layer the crêpes and pomelo cream until the top of the ring is reached. Sprinkle with powdered sugar. Refrigerate for 45 minutes before unmolding and serving.

Spiced Fennel

For the candied fennel:
6 bulbs of fennel
6½ tbsp/100 g sugar
3½ tbsp/50 g butter
2½ cupst/600 ml water
2 star anise
a pinch of cardamom
a pinch of mixed pepper
¼ of a licorice stick

For the pastry cream:
  (see basic recipe)
1 cup/250 ml milk
3 egg yolks
¼ cup/60 g sugar
1 vanilla bean
1 star anise

For the nougatine:
½ cup/125 g butter
1¾ oz/50 g dextrose
½ cup plus 2 tbsp/150 g sugar
¾ cup/90 g sliced almonds
¾ cup/90 g green pistachios

For the garnish:
a few green pistachios

Serves   6
Preparation time: 40 minutes
Cooking time: 35 minutes
Difficulty: ★ ★

Originally from Italy, the aromatic nuances of fennel are now enjoyed worldwide. It is usually eaten as a vegetable. Here, however, its anise-like flavor blends with our chef's selection of spices to create an extraordinary dessert.

The fennel should be candied in a water-and-sugar-based syrup, simmering slowly over very low heat. The cooking time depends on the size of the fennel and can vary anywhere from 10 to 60 minutes. The fennel must be thoroughly drained after being candied. To dry the fennel properly, place it on a cookie sheet, sprinkle it with confectioners' sugar and cover with a sheet of wax paper. Cover it with another cookie sheet and bake at 210 °F/100 °C while closely monitoring the fennel to make sure that it retains its original shape.

Our chef advises against filling the nougat with cream too far in advance to prevent it from becoming soggy. For an eyecatching garnish, some of the nougat can be used to make a bow for the top of the dessert. If the nougat hardens before the bow is finished, it can be put in the oven for a few seconds to soften. If desired, a slice of candied or dried orange, lemon or pineapple can be used for decoration.

This dessert will impress everyone, and no one will guess how simple it was to prepare.

1. Prepare the fennel by removing its branches and use only the bulb-like bottoms. In a pot, combine all the ingredients for the candying. Add the fennel, cover and let simmer for 15 minutes. Prick with a paring knife to determine if the fennel is done.

2. Prepare the pastry cream as described in the basic recipe but substituting the ingredients listed above. Cook for 5 minutes. Fill the candied fennel with some of the pastry cream. Place the stuffed fennel on a plate and set aside. Reserve the remaining pastry cream to fill the nougat.

Nougat

3. To make the nougat, melt the butter and add the dextrose and sugar. Stir over low heat for 5 minutes. Remove from the heat and add the almonds and coarsely chopped pistachios. Spread this mixture on a non-stick cookie sheet and bake for 5 to 10 minutes at 390 °F/200 °C until golden brown.

4. Remove the nougatine from the oven and let cool a few seconds. While it is still warm and malleable, mold it in the shape of a large, hollow flower. Fill the nougat with the remaining pastry cream and delicately place the stuffed fennel inside it. Sprinkle a few pistachios over the fennel and serve.

Mango

For the puff pastry:
(see basic recipe)
1⅔ cups/200 g flour
6½ tbsp/100 ml water
10 tbsp/150 g butter
a pinch of salt

For the filling:
½ cup/250 g strawberries
3½ tbsp/50 ml grenadine
1 large mango
3½ tbsp/50 ml yellow curaçao
5 tsp candied lemon peel

For the cream mixture:
2 cups/500 ml heavy cream
6½ tbsp/50 g confectioners' sugar
3½ oz/100 g cream cheese
2 vanilla beans

For the garnish:
¼ cup/30 g confectioners' sugar
1 lemon
1 strawberry
1 slice of mango

Serves	*6*
Preparation time:	*1 hour 15 minutes*
Cooking time:	*40 minutes*
Chilling time:	*2 hours*
Difficulty:	★ ★

The famous painter Claude Gellée, known as Le Lorrain, began his career as a pastry sous-chef and claimed that he invented puff pastry! At the same time, a certain Feuillet, pastry chef for the Prince of Condé, claimed that only he had truly developed the special relationship between butter and pastry. No matter how this matter is resolved, one must simply try this wonderful millefeuille for oneself.

Gently fragrant and filled with the most delicate creams, flavored with mango, strawberry and lemon, this millefeuille is a sweet, tangy treat.

Other fruits can can easily be substituted in this recipe. They should be ripe but firm. Possible variations include grapefruit instead of lemon, guava for mango and any red fruit in place of strawberry. The garnish should be changed to represent the fruits used in the millefeuille.

Puff pastry can be purchased instead of making it from scratch. If it is store-bought it should not be kneaded as this will ruin the light texture.

If you are creatively inclined, one corner of the millefeuille can be elegantly decorated with fruit slices and mint leaves as pictured here. Candied lemon, easily prepared by cooking lemon slices in sugar syrup (see basic recipes), will blend beautifully with the slices of fresh fruit.

1. Prepare the puff pastry as described in the basic recipe but substituting the ingredients listed above. Roll it out and let it rest on a buttered cookie sheet for 30 minutes. Bake for 20 minutes at 355 °F/180 °C. Beat the heavy cream with the confectioners' sugar. Beat in the cream cheese and the seeds of the vanilla beans.

2. Dice the strawberries and fold into one-third of the cream, then stir in the grenadine to add color. Dice the mango and fold into another third of the cream, and then yellow curaçao and the candied lemon peel to the final third.

Millefeuille

3. Cut the baked puff pastry into 4 identical triangles.

4. Spread each type of cream on 1 of the triangles. Put the millefeuille together and cover with the last triangle. Sprinkle with confectioners' sugar and garnish with lemon slices, strawberries, mango and fresh mint leaves. Refrigerate for 2 hours.

Orange

For the filling:
5 oranges
6½ tbsp/100 ml water
6½ tbsp/100 g sugar
6½ tbsp/100 ml grenadine
a few grains of black pepper
a few grains of coriander
8 sheets of gelatin
4 egg whites
1 tsp butter

For the sweet short pastry:
  (see basic recipe)
1⅔ cups/200 g flour
6½ tbsp/100 g sugar
6½ tbsp/100 g butter
2 eggs
a pinch of salt

For the garnish:
1 orange
1 leaf of fresh mint

Serves	*8*
Preparation time:	*2 hours 30 minutes*
Cooking time:	*1 hour 20 minutes*
Chilling time:	*1 hour 30 minutes*
Difficulty:	★ ★

Coriander seeds, which resemble grains of pepper, can easily be grown into fresh coriander by letting the grains germinate in a few inches of soil with a little fertilizer. It will only take about six weeks to see the stems appear. The popularity of fresh coriander is growing, and it is no longer a rarity in supermarkets. It is replacing parsley more and more in salads and dishes, which gives a new twist to many classic recipes.

To slice a fruit or vegetable *à la julienne* means to slice thin, matchstick-like pieces. The zest from most citrus fruits keeps fairly well. If only the juice of a fruit is being used, remove the zest before squeezing it. The zest should be cut to julienne, blanched and dried, then simmered in sugar syrup for 30 minutes. Once this is done, the candied zest should be placed on a cookie sheet and dried in the oven at very low heat.

The candied zest will come in handy for many different dessert recipes. Some people even enjoy eating it as a snack, despite its strong taste.

A prebaked crust that contains a moist filling such as a pastry cream or jelly will often become soggy. To prevent this, the crust can be covered with a thin layer of melted butter which will "waterproof" it.

1. Remove the zest from 3 of the oranges with a peeler and slice it into julienne. Blanch in simmering water and then drain. Simmer the julienned zest and the zest of a fourth orange in the water with half the sugar, the grenadine, pepper and coriander for about 50 minutes or until all the water has evaporated.

2. Reserve a little zest for the garnish. Prepare a sweet short pastry as instructed in the basic recipe, but substituting the ingredients listed above. Let it rest 30 minutes, then roll it out and fit into a pan. Bake it twice, for 15 minutes each time, at 390 °F/200 °C. Brush melted butter on the crust when it is removed from the oven.

Pepper Pie

3. Juice all 5 oranges. Dissolve the gelatin in ½ cup of the juice and a little water. Pour the dissolved gelatin back into the rest of the juice. Let it cool until it has begun to solidify. Beat the egg whites until very firm and add the remaining sugar. Fold the zest and juice into the egg whites.

4. Pour the filling into the pie crust. Garnish with the remaining zest. Refrigerate for 1½ hours before serving.

Chocolate

For the shortbread:
(see basic recipe)
1⅔ cups/200 g flour
6½ tbsp/100 g butter
2 eggs
3½ tbsp/50 g sugar
a pinch of salt

For the chocolate-coffee cream:
½ cup/125 g sugar
10 egg yolks

2 cups/500 ml heavy cream
1 cup/250 ml milk
6 tbsp/25 g instant coffee
¼ cup/30 g powdered cocoa

For the custard:
(see basic recipe)
1 cup/250 ml milk
3 egg yolks
8 tsp/40 g sugar
1 vanilla bean

Serves	*6*
Preparation time:	*1 hour*
Cooking time:	*55 minutes*
Chilling time:	*1 hour*
Difficulty:	★ ★

The origin of coffee is unclear, but it is believed to have come from the Sudan or Ethiopia. The invention of coffee as a drink and the discovery of its stimulating qualities are the subject of several myths. Some credit this discovery to a shepherd who noticed that his goats became agitated when they ate the leaves of coffee shrubs. Cocoa is the fruit of the cacao tree, which, according to one legend, was the most beautiful tree of the Aztec paradise. If this is true, then its origin must then be Mexican. Cocoa was certainly a stimulant for the Spanish conquerors. The Spanish sweetened the cocoa because they did not like its bitter taste. To this day, sugar cane plantations often border cocoa plantations.

Care must be taken in filling the crust. The chocolate-coffee filling is very liquid and can easily spill out when putting it in the oven. One trick to prevent this potential catastrophe is to pull the oven rack out halfway and place the empty crust in the oven. Then the filling can be poured into the crust. Shortbread, like most doughs, should not be over-handled. This will make it rubbery and cause it to shrink as it bakes.

This Chocolate Coffee Brick, sprinkled with confectioners' sugar just before serving, can be served with a vanilla custard. To have a ready supply of vanilla sugar available, just drop two vanilla beans in a sealed jar of sugar and let the sugar take on their flavor over time.

1. Make a well in the flour and place the sliced, softened butter in the center. Lightly rub the flour and butter together between the palms of your hands. Add the eggs, sugar and salt. Knead the dough into a ball and let it rest for 30 minutes.

2. Roll out the dough. Fit it into a buttered pan and prick it with a fork. Cover with wax paper and weigh it down with dried beans. Bake for 12 minutes at 390 °F/200 °C. Remove the wax paper and the beans and bake for an additional 2 or 3 minutes.

Coffee Brick

3. Make the chocolate-coffee cream by beating the egg yolks with the sugar. Boil the milk and the cream with the instant coffee and cocoa. Pour the hot milk mixture into the eggs while stirring vigorously.

4. Pour the filling into the crust and bake at 210 °F/100 °C for 30–40 minutes. Refrigerate for 1 hour and serve with custard (see basic recipe).

Chocolate and Vanilla

2 large prickly pears
3½ tbsp/50 g sugar
2 tbsp/30 g butter
6½ tbsp/50 g confectioners' sugar

For the pastry cream:
  (see basic recipe)
5 tbsp/75 g sugar
3 egg yolks
1 cup/250 ml milk
1 vanilla bean

For the puff pastry:
  (see basic recipe)
2 cups/250 g flour
½ cup/125 ml water
a pinch of salt
¾ cup/180 g butter
1 egg

For the chocolate coating:
5¼ oz/150 g dark chocolate
3½ tbsp/50 g butter
1⅔ cups/400 ml heavy cream

Serves   4
Preparation time: 1 hour
Cooking time: 33 minutes
Chilling time: 5 minutes
Difficulty: ★ ★

Prickly pears grow on thick trees all around the Mediterranean. Their yellow-orange pulp is fresh, slightly acidic and full of crunchy seeds. The skin is thick and covered in small thorns. Whether it is eaten raw or cooked, the thorns should always be removed. This can be accomplished by rubbing the prickly pear with a thick dish towel, being careful to wear gloves!

The number of petals can be changed to accomodate the number of guests, though no more than six should be made at one time. When brushing on the egg yolk, it is important not to let any drip from the pastry to the cookie sheet. This would prevent the pastry from rising in that area. Our chef suggests using only very good quality chocolate (70% cocoa content) for the coating. To conserve the expensive chocolate the seared pears can be set on a rack over tin foil or wax paper and the chocolate poured on them. The excess chocolate that has run off the pears can be reused. This chocolate coating is not difficult to make, but to save time and money, very good chocolate dips can be found in the supermarket.

A slice of strawberry or a drop of white chocolate are also excellent choices for garnishing the pears.

1. Prepare the pastry cream as describe in the basic recipe but substituting the ingredients listed above. Peel the prickly pears and slice them in half. Sauté them in a pan with the butter for about 8 minutes. Prepare the puff pastry as described in the basic recipe, again using the ingredients listed above. Let it rest 3 times for 20 minutes each time.

2. Cut out a flower shape from the puff pastry. Cut out the center of each petal but do not remove it from the petal. Brush egg yolk on the pastry and bake on a cookie sheet at 390 °F/200 °C for 15 minutes on a cookie sheet. Remove the center of the petals and place elsewhere on the cookie sheet. Sprinkle all with confectioners' sugar and bake an additional 5 minutes to brown.

Prickly Pear Petals

3. For the coating, melt the chocolate and butter in a double boiler. Vigorously stir in the cream. Spear a pear on the end of a fork and coat it with chocolate. Repeat with the 3 others. Refrigerate for 5 minutes to set the chocolate.

4. Spread the cold pastry cream into the holes in the petals. Cover the pears in a second coat of chocolate and place them on the pastry cream. Delicately arrange the centers of the petals on the cream. Serve immediately.

St. Lucian

For the egg-white pastry:
1⅔ cups/200 g flour
6½ tbsp/100 g butter
a pinch of salt
1¼ cup/300 ml water

For the filling:
1 lb/500 g mango
1 egg

3½ tbsp/50 g sugar
6½ tbsp/100 ml orange-flavored liqueur
2 sheets of gelatin
½ cup water

For the whipped cream:
6½ tbsp/100 ml whipping cream
8 tsp/40 g sugar

Serves	*6*
Preparation time:	*50 minutes*
Cooking time:	*30 minutes*
Difficulty:	★ ★

Pie, a cornerstone of Anglo-Saxon culinary art, can have a sweet or savory filling. The quintessential pie for many people is, of course, apple pie. Now independent, St. Lucia was once part of the Commonwealth, and this recipe is inspired by British cooking. The mango pie presents no real difficulty but requires careful attention when fitting the dough into the mold. The crust should be filled to 1 in/2 cm from the top. One teaspoon of water added to an egg yolk will make a good glaze to brush the top of the pastry as well as to seal the top crust to the pie shell.

Pressing the edges firmly will ensure that the pie is well-sealed. As the pie bakes, the juice from the mangoes will give off steam, which may cause the crust to burst. If the top of the pie is browning too quickly, cover it with foil.

This dessert can be eaten hot or cold. Gelatin should only be used if the pie is to be served cold, since it will only set if chilled. If the pie is being served warm, the natural flavor of the fruit will be sweet enough, so leave out the sugar for the whipped cream.

1. Prepare the pastry by combining the flour, softened butter, salt and water. Let it rest 30 minutes. Roll out ⅔ of the pastry, prick it with a fork and fit it into a mold or pie plate.

2. Peel and pit the mangoes, then dice them. Sauté them quickly with the sugar and flambé them with the liqueur. Dissolve the gelatin in a little water and add it to the fruit.

Mango Pie

3. Fill the crust with the fruit. Make a top crust for the pie with the rest of the pastry. Brush some egg yolk around the edges of the pie and on the top crust. Press the edges together very tightly. Bake at 430 °F/220 °C for 10 minutes, then at 355 °F/180 °C for 20 minutes.

4. Let the pie cool and unmold it gently. Cut the top off and pour the whipped cream into the pie. Close the pie before serving either warm or cold.

Banana and

For the short pastry:
(see basic recipe)
2 cups/250 g flour
½ cup/125 g butter
1 egg
1 tbsp water
1 vanilla bean
2 tbsp/30 g sugar

For the filling:
2 lb 3 oz/1 kg bananas
1 lemon
4 cloves
1 egg yolk
⅓ cup/100 g honey
3½ tbsp/50 g brown sugar
a pinch of pepper
2 tbsp water
6½ tbsp/100 ml heavy cream

Serves   4
Preparation time: 30 minutes
Cooking time: 45 minutes
Difficulty: ★

This wonderful pie combines the sweetness of honey and sugar with the spiciness of cloves and pepper, and is sure to spark the curiosity of any guest.

Our chef has chosen bananas, but apples, guava or mango could be used just as easily. It is essential to use firm fruit. If the fruit is too juicy or ripe, it will make the pastry crust soggy.

The clove and pepper can be replaced by vanilla or cardamom for variation.

The "chimney" in the center of the pie will allow the steam to escape and prevent the dough from losing its consistency. As it cooks, the juice released by the bananas may overflow and leave traces on the top of the pie.

The spiced caramel, which contains pepper, will be enhanced by a few drops of dark rum. When adding the cream to the caramel, one should be very careful to avoid being burnt by the steam.

If the caramel seems too thick, additional cream can be added by simply pouring it through the "chimney" so that it coats the bananas.

1. Prepare the short pastry as described in the basic recipe, but substituting the ingredients listed above. Let it rest for 30 minutes. Roll it out and fit it into a high-sided baking dish. Slice the bananas, juice the lemon, and grind the cloves. Then combine all 3 ingredients in a metal mixing bowl. Fill the pie crust with this mixture.

2. Make a top crust for the pie and cut a vent in the middle.

Spiced Honey Pie

3. Cover the pie with the top crust. The edges should be well-sealed. Brush the top with a lightly beaten egg and garnish it with the point of a knife. Bake for 30 minutes at 390 °F/200 °C.

4. Prepare the caramel with the honey, brown sugar, pepper and water. Deglaze the pan with the cream and stir this into the caramel. Pour the caramel mixture into the "chimney" as soon as the pie is removed from the oven.

Asian Pear

For the dough:
2 cups/250 g flour
a pinch of salt
½ cup/125 g butter
1 egg

For the filling:
2 Asian pears
1 tbsp passion fruit liqueur
3½ tbsp/50 g sugar
1 tsp butter
a few pinches of pepper
1 egg

Serves	*4*
Preparation time:	*45 minutes*
Cooking time:	*50 minutes*
Difficulty:	*★*

Asian pears originate from Japan and are grown in Australia and New Zealand. They are exported around the world. This round fruit, which closely resembles a Golden Delicious apple, has a texture very similar to that of a pear. Juicy, sweet and flavorful, it contains many minerals and vitamins. It can be eaten alone or made into jelly or jam, juice or fruit salad. It also serves as a good accompaniment to meat or fish dishes.

With its similarities to both fruits, Asian pear is easily replaced by apples or pears. Only the cooking times must be changed. The classic turnover with flavors of pear and pepper is traditionally served hot, but with this exotic variation our chef has chosen to serve it warm. It is even delicious cold.

To seal the turnover in a creative way, the edge is rolled by hand. It is then sliced with the tip of a knife at regular intervals to add an extra dimension.

To give the turnover an even more glamorous look, it can be decorated by etching designs on the top with a knife. However, one must be careful to not cut through the dough, which would allow the fruit to seep out.

1. Place the flour in a bowl and make a well. Add the salt, the softened butter and the egg. Quickly knead the dough and let it rest 1 hour. Peel and core the pears and dice them. Save the pear skin for the garnish. Marinate the fruit in the liqueur for 30 minutes.

2. Season the pears with a few pinches of pepper. Sauté them in the butter and sugar for about 10 minutes. Roll out the dough to a thickness of ¼ in/5 mm. Make an oval shape with it which will allow room to fold it over the fruit and form the turnover.

Turnover

3. Drain the pears in a strainer and place them on the dough. Brush a beaten egg along the edges of the dough and seal it.

4. Shape the edges of the pastry. Brush the remaining egg on the top of the turnover and bake for 40 minutes at 410 °F/210 °C. After 10 minutes lower the temperature to 355 °F/180 °C. Serve warm.

Gingerbread and

8¾ oz/250 g gingerbread

For the custard filling:
1 cup/250 ml milk
1 vanilla bean
2 eggs
1 tbsp sugar
3 tbsp dark rum

For the short pastry:
   (see basic recipe)
1⅔ cups/200 g flour
2 eggs

a pinch of salt
3½ tbsp/50 g sugar
1 vanilla bean
6½ tbsp/100 g butter

For the fruit filling:
¾ cup/125 g raisins
1¼ cups/200 g candied citron peels

For the garnish:
1 egg
6½ tbsp/50 g confectioners' sugar (optional)

Serves	6
Preparation time:	1 hour
Cooking time:	45 minutes
Chilling time:	2 hours
Difficulty:	★ ★

Citron has a thick rind and is rarely eaten raw because it has little juice. Usually, only its rind is used in pastries and even then it is often candied. It is well-suited to this dessert recipe since the oranges, grapefruit, lemons, mandarins or kumquats are tart enough to balance out the sweetness of the raisins and the gingerbread.

Our chef suggests mincing the candied citron as small as possible. This will make slicing the pie much easier. Either regular raisins or white raisins can be used. Even seedless grapes are an option, but an extra egg must then be added to the filling. Two sheets of gelatin can be added as well to make sure the custard is firm and ensure an attractive finished product.

Our chef suggests simply serving the pie in the pan, but it can also be inverted. In this case, one should not make a "chimney" in the top crust.

Painting the top of the crust with a lightly beaten egg before baking and dusting it with confectioners' sugar just before serving will add an attractive touch.

1. Cut the gingerbread into ¼ in/5 mm thick slices. For the custard filling, warm the milk with the vanilla. When it begins to simmer remove from heat. Beat the eggs with the sugar and rum. Pour the hot milk into the eggs, mix well, and briefly soak the gingerbread slices in this mixture.

2. Prepare the short pastry as described in the basic recipe but substituting the ingredients listed above. Butter a 7 in/18 cm pan with high sides and fit the dough into it. Save enough dough to make a top crust for the pie. Line the bottom of the pie shell with a few slices of soaked gingerbread.

Fruit Custard Pie

3. Alternately add layers of raisins, candied zest and gingerbread. The last layer should be gingerbread, which can be crushed into crumbs.

4. Pour the remaining egg mixture from Step 1 into the pie. Cover with the top crust and brush it with a beaten egg. Make a "chimney" in the center and seal the edges. Brush the pie with egg again. Bake for 10 minutes at 390 °F/200 °C and then for 35 minutes at 320 °F/160 °C. Cool, then refrigerate for 2 hours. Unmold and sprinkle with confectioners' sugar if desired.

Papaya and

2 papayas

For the sweet short pastry:
2 egg yolks
6½ tbsp/100 g sugar
a pinch of salt
1⅔ cups/200 g flour
½ cup/60 g ground hazelnuts
6½ tbsp/100 g butter
3½ tbsp/50 ml water

For the filling:
6½ tbsp/100 ml milk
6½ tbsp/100 ml whipping cream
½ cup passion fruit liqueur
¼ cup/60 g sugar
2 eggs

Serves	*6*
Preparation time:	*1 hour*
Cooking time:	*45 minutes*
Chilling time:	*1 hour*
Difficulty:	★

Hazelnut trees play an important role in the culture of many tropical countries. Because their branches are so supple, they were often used by diviners to find underground water sources. Finding water was a vital skill and talented dowsers were famous thoughout their region. Thus hazelnut trees were valued both for their branches and their tasty nuts in many societies.

The papaya tree resembles a palm tree. It is also known as the "melon tree" since papayas contain many seeds, just like melons. Because of an enzyme found in papayas, they are very easy to digest and can be eaten in great quantities. When the papaya is ripe, its flesh is very soft and melts in the mouth. This consistency unfortunately also makes the papaya difficult to handle. In this recipe, barely ripe papayas should be chosen, to make slicing them easier.

Pears or mangoes, because they have the same shape as papaya, can easily be used as a substitute.

A few whole, roasted hazelnut can be sprinkled on the finished quiche, if desired.

1. To make the pastry, beat the egg yolks with the sugar and salt. Stir in the flour, hazelnuts and butter. Knead in the water. Form the dough into a ball and let it rest 30 minutes. Roll it out and prick it with a fork.

2. Pit and peel the papayas, then slice them lengthwise.

Hazelnut Quiche

3. Place the pastry in a buttered pie pan. Bake twice, for 10 minutes each time, at 390 °F/200 °C. Once cooled, arrange the papayas in the pastry shell.

4. For the filling, combine the milk, cream, liqueur and sugar. Whisk in the eggs. Pour the filling over the papayas and bake for 25 minutes at 390 °F/200 °C. Refrigerate for 1 hour. Serve cool.

Tomato

For the shortbread:
(see basic recipe)
2 cups/250 g flour
½ cup/125 g butter
5 tsp sugar

For the almond cream:
½ cup/125 g butter
1 cup/125 g finely ground almonds
1 cup/125 g confectioners' sugar
1 tbsp/15 g cornstarch
2 eggs
1 vanilla bean

Serves	*6*
Preparation time:	*1 hour 10 minutes*
Cooking time:	*50 minutes*
Chilling time:	*1 hour*
Difficulty:	★ ★ ★

For the tomatoes:
7 small tomatoes
2 tsp rum
¼ cup/30 g raisins
1 dried fig
6 walnuts
3 tbsp/30 g candied citron
1 tsp orange-flavored liqueur
2 tbsp/20 g coarsely chopped hazelnuts
3 tbsp/30 g candied kumquats
3 tbsp/30 g candied orange peel

For the caramel:
½ cup plus 2 tbsp/150 g sugar
2 cups/500 ml water

This spectacular tomato dessert demands minute attention to detail in its preparation. The shortbread can be baked in advance. It can even be made the day before, as the tomatoes will require a great deal of attention.

Our chef offers a time-consuming but delicious recommendation concerning the tomato stuffing. Fill each one with almond cream blended with one of the following combinations of ingredients: rum and raisins, walnuts and dried figs, candied citron and orange-flavored liqueur, hazelnuts and candied kumquats, rum and candied orange rind, and one with the almond cream alone. The final tomato should be stuffed with a medley of all these ingredients. Of course, this recipe can be simplified by using only two or three of these items. Bright red tomatoes should be chosen so that even if they lose some of their color as they bake, they will still be vivid.

A glaze for the tomatoes will help preserve their appearance. Simply reduce the liquid used in boiling the tomatoes. For the garnish, pistachios can be used, as well as fresh mint leaves, citronella leaves, hyssop leaves or a slice of carambola as pictured here.

This elaborate presentation will bring many compliments to the chef and impress any guest with its delicate taste and attractive appearance.

1. Prepare the shortbread as described in the basic recipe but substituting the ingredients listed above. Let it rest for 30 minutes. For the almond cream, soften the butter, then combine all the ingredients. Set half aside. Divide the remaining half into seven even portions

3. Peel, seed and drain the tomatoes. Carmelize the sugar and water in a pan.

Profiterole Tart

3. Roll out the shortbread. Cut out a circle, and crimp around the edges. Bake it for 15 minutes at 390 °F/200 °C. Once cooled, cover it with the reserved almond cream. Bake for another 10 minutes at 390 °F/200 °C. Prepare the 7 different creams as described in the text, and stuff each tomato.

4. Pour the caramel into an oven-proof baking dish, set the filled tomatoes on the caramel, and bake for 25 minutes at 355 °F/180 °C. Baste the tomatoes with the caramel as they bake. Once cooled, wrap each one individually in plastic wrap and refrigerate for 1 hour. Place them on the tart and garnish with the remaining tomato sauce.

Coconut Shortbread with

1 mango

For the coconut shortbread:
1 tbsp grated ginger
1 tbsp sugar
½ cup/125 g sugar
½ cup/125 g butter
2 eggs
2 cups/250 g flour
½ cup plus 1 tbsp/50 g grated coconut

Serves | 6
Preparation time: | 1 hour
Cooking time: | 20 minutes
Chilling time: | 2 hours
Difficulty: | ★ ★

For the pistachio mousse:
4 egg yolks
8 tsp/40 g sugar
8 tsp/20 g cornstarch
2 sheets of gelatin
½ cup water
1 cup/250 ml heavy cream
4 tsp/20 g pistachio paste or
  ¾ cup/100 g chopped green pistachios
1 cup/250 ml milk

For the garnish:
1½ tbsp/30 g apricot jelly
a few leaves of fresh mint

Ginger is a root which has many uses, bringing a subtle yet distinctive flavor to any dessert. By simply mixing a little ginger with some sugar, one can liven up a pastry or melon which has a too-mild flavor.

To grate the ginger root more easily, it can be soaked in cold water for a few minutes without lessening its nutritional qualities. In this recipe, our chef has candied the ginger by mincing it finely and combining it with a small amount of water and 1 tablespoon of sugar. The ginger is then simmered for 25 minutes. The sugar can also be replaced with honey.

The shortbread used here can be replaced by sponge cake or slightly leavened dough, as described in the basic recipes. A store bought sponge cake will save time.

For those who like to add a little zing, our chef has used pistachio paste to lend the mousse an intense pistachio flavor. Otherwise, ground pistachios should be boiled in milk (about ¾ cup milk per 100 g pistachios). This step is more time-consuming, but will result in a much more delicate dessert. The pistachios can also be omitted from the mousse entirely.

1. Candy the ginger as described. Make the shortbread by combining the sugar and butter. Add the eggs one at a time, then the flour, coconut and candied ginger. Allow the dough to rest in a cool place for 30 minutes, then roll it out and cut out 2 pieces of the same shape. Bake for 20 minutes at 355 °F/180 °C.

2. For the pistachio mousse, beat the egg yolks with the sugar and add the cornstarch. Bring this to a boil. Dissolve the gelatin in a little water. Remove the egg from the heat and stir in the gelatin and pistachio paste or ground pistachios boiled in the milk. Whip the cream and fold it gently into the mousse.

Pistachio Cream and Mango

3. In the same mold used to cut out the dough, place 1 layer of the baked shortbread and pour in the mousse. Refrigerate for 2 hours. Unmold and place the second piece of shortbread on top.

4. Peel and slice the mango. Arrange the slices attractively on top of the pie. Brush with warmed apricot jelly and add a leaf of mint and some pistachios as garnish.

Belle Créole

2 lb 3 oz/1 kg melon
2 tbsp/30 g brown sugar
a pinch of curry

For the short pastry:
(see basic recipe)
1⅖ cups/200 g flour
6½ tbsp/100 g butter
1 egg
2 tbsp water
1 vanilla bean
3½ tbsp/50 g sugar
a pinch of salt

Serves	6
Preparation time:	1 hour
Cooking time:	40 minutes
Chilling time:	15 minutes
Difficulty:	★

For the pastry cream:
(see basic recipe)
1 cup/250 ml milk
5 tbsp/70 g sugar
2 tbsp plus 1 tsp/20 g flour
1 tbsp/10 g cornstarch
2 egg yolks
1 vanilla bean
a pinch of curry

For the topping and garnish:
10½ oz/250 g dark chocolate
3 tbsp water
4 tsp/20 ml orange-flavored liqueur

Belle Hélène is the term used in pastry-making for chocolate covered fruits, and here our chef has created a Belle Créole, using the same concept with a Carribean flair.

Melons need a warm climate which helps them ripen and develop. However, after a melon has been, picked it should not be exposed to heat. Once melons are harvested they are stored in cool, shady places and are shipped in refrigerated containers. At home melon can be kept at room temperature or in the refrigerator. If refrigerated, it should not stay there too long as its strong aroma will spread to the other foods in the refrigerator. Melon is often sliced and eaten as a dessert. This melon pie must be made the same day it is served or the melon juices will tend to make the crust soggy.

Our chef is among those who believes that there is no such thing as too much chocolate, and assures us that the quantities given here can be increased as desired without adverse effect.

Fresh figs can be used instead of melon; however, in this case the pie will need to bake about 15 minutes longer at 355 °F/180 °C for the figs to ensure that they cook fully before they are covered with chocolate.

Arrange the chocolate lace in the center of the pie and serve it well-chilled.

1. Prepare a short pastry as described in the basic recipe but substituting the ingredients listed above. Let it rest for 30 minutes, then roll it out and prick with a fork. Fit it into a pan. Bake twice for 15 minutes each time at 390 °F/200 °C. Prepare the pastry cream as described in the basic recipe again using the ingredients listed above. Fill the crust with the pastry cream.

2. Peel the melon and cut it into slices. Let them drain on a rack and then sprinkle with a little brown sugar combined with curry. Arrange the melon slices on the pastry cream.

Pie

3. Melt the chocolate in a double boiler with the water and liqueur. Partially cover the melon with the chocolate and set the remaining chocolate aside.

4. Using a homemade pastry bag (make a cone out of wax paper and snip off the tip), draw lace designs with the melted chocolate on wax paper. Refrigerate for 15 minutes and garnish the pie with the hardened lace just before serving.

Caged

For the pastry cream:
(see basic recipe)
1 cup/250 ml milk
¼ cup/60 g sugar
4 tsp/10 g flour
2 tsp/5 g cornstarch
1 vanilla bean
1 egg yolk

For the shortbread:
(see basic recipe)
1⅔ cups/200 g flour
6½ tbsp/100 g butter
a pinch of salt
3–4 tbsp water

For the filling:
3½ tbsp/50 ml litchi liqueur
3 cups/1 barquette cape gooseberries
⅓ cup/50 g raisins
⅓ cup/100–125 g mango jelly

Serves	*6*
Preparation time:	*45 minutes*
Cooking time:	*35 minutes*
Chilling time:	*1 hour*
Difficulty:	★

The cape gooseberry has several different names, and one of the slang terms for it in French means "caged love." Its flesh is very juicy and crunchy. It has almost as much vitamin A as persimmon, and also has a good deal of vitamin C.

The Portuguese made this connection early on and began cultivating the cape gooseberry in diverse strategic locations, such as the Cape of Good Hope, where their ships would anchor and the sailors would gather large quantities of the berries. This helped their sailors fight off scurvy, a disease caused by a lack of vitamin C.

Cape gooseberries are only edible when ripe. The berry should be yellow, not green. Unripe berries can even be harmful. The cape gooseberry is a very simple fruit and is used in jams or can be dipped in chocolate. Litchi liqueur is very smooth and will nicely balance out the slight acidity of the cape gooseberry. However, other liqueurs may be substituted.

The pastry and pastry cream used in this recipe can be flavored with several different ingredients, such as mango and papaya. But it is the cape gooseberry that makes this Caged Love Pie unique.

1. Soak the raisins in the litchi liqueur. Prepare the pastry cream as described in the basic recipe but substituting the ingredients listed above. Stir the marinated raisins into the pastry cream.

2. Prepare the shortbread as described in the basic recipe using the ingredients listed above. Roll it out and fit the shortbread into a pie pan. Bake twice for 15 minutes each time at 390 °F/200 °C. Remove the the papery outer skin from the berries and slice each berry in half.

Love Pie

3. Pour the pastry cream into the crust and carefully arrange each half berry on the cream so that the sliced side is facing up. Bake for 5 minutes at 390 °F/200 °C. Let cool.

4. Warm the mango jelly slightly. When it has melted a little, brush the top of the pie with it. Refrigerate for 1 hour. Unmold and serve cold.

Orange

1 lb/500 g oranges
½ cup/150 g guava jelly
2 tbsp butter

For the short pastry:
(see basic recipe)
2 cups/200 g flour
½ cup/120 g butter
1 egg
a pinch of salt
3½ tbsp/50 g sugar
1 vanilla bean

For the pastry cream:
(see basic recipe)
2 cups/500 ml milk
½ cup/125 g sugar
3½ tbsp/25 g flour
2 tbsp/15 g cornstarch
3 egg yolks

Serves	*6*
Preparation time:	*30 minutes*
Cooking time:	*35 minutes*
Chilling time:	*30 minutes*
Difficulty:	★

It is often taken for granted, but it is extraordinary the way that cooking transforms raw ingredients. Cooking modifies the consistency of a food, alters its appearance and develops its aromas and flavors.

Prebaking a crust covered in tin foil and weighed down with dried beans will prevent the pastry from rising and losing its shape. Once the tin foil and weights are removed, the crust will finish baking and browning.

Regardless of the fruit chosen for this recipe, the crust should always be brushed with a little melted butter in order to "waterproof" it. This way, if the fruit gives off juices, the crust will not become soggy. The basic pastry cream used here can be livened up with a little orange zest, which should be soaked in milk previously.

The best way to carve the sections from the orange is to use a long, sharp knife. This will allow for greater precision.

Pomelo or mandarins can be used here rather than oranges. Lemon and lime should not be used since the acidity of their juice could curdle the milk.

Why not try this refreshing dessert at dinner tonight?

1. Prepare the short pastry as described in the basic recipe but substituting the ingredients listed above. Let it rest for 30 minutes, then roll it out and fit it into a pan. Bake it twice for 10 minutes each time. After removing it from the oven, brush some melted butter on the crust.

2. Peel the oranges, saving one for the garnish. Section the oranges, removing all the membranes. Prepare the pastry cream as described in the basic recipe but using the ingredients listed above. Refrigerate it for 30 minutes.

Pie

3. Slice the remaining orange. Fill the crust with a layer of pastry cream. Lie the orange sections on the cream and smother them with the remaining pastry cream.

4. Attractively arrange a few sections on the top of the pie with one slice in the middle. Use the guava jelly to glaze the top; candied fruit can also be added to the garnish.

Orange

¼ cup/50 g guava jelly

Sponge cake: (see basic recipe)

For the short pastry: (see basic recipe)
½ cup/125 g butter
1⅗ cups/200 g flour
1 egg
1 tbsp water
a pinch of salt
1 vanilla bean
3½ tbsp/50 g sugar

For the pastry cream:
5 eggs
3 egg yolks
¾ cup plus 1 tbsp/200 g sugar
¾ cup/200 ml orange juice
zest of 3 oranges
13 tbsp/200 g butter
⅔ cup/150 ml orange-flavored liqueur

For the candied oranges:
1⅗ cups/400 ml sugar syrup
(see basic recipe)
1 orange

Serves	*6*
Preparation time:	*40 minutes*
Cooking time:	*1 hour 45 minutes*
Chilling time:	*1 hour*
Difficulty:	★

Sponge cake can be kept for up to three days in the refrigerator, and as long as two months in the freezer. According to our chef, sponge cake made a day in advance is easier to cut and soaks up flavoring much more readily than freshly-baked cake. Store bought sponge cake or lady fingers can also be substituted.

For this recipe, our chef suggests that the flour be added quickly to avoid overworking the batter. Also, one should try and encorporate more air into the batter while mixing. To give the sponge cake an even lighter consistency a packet of yeast may be added. One way to test if the sponge cake is done is to listen for the very faint sound it will make when it is tapped lightly. There should be a small squeak. Let the cake cool in its pan. It will shrink as it cools, making it easier to remove. In this pie, the sponge cake will be soaked in orange-flavored liqueur, which will make it very moist. The orange pastry cream will add a wonderful, fresh flavor to the pie. If the cream seems too loose, a little flour should be added to thicken it.

To accentuate the color of this dessert, a little zest of lime can be placed on top: A perfect touch for an Orange Cream Pie!

1. Prepare the sponge cake according to the basic recipe, adding the flour quickly. Pour the batter in a buttered and floured pan and bake at 390 °F/200 °C for 15 minutes.

2. Prepare the short pastry as described in the basic recipe but substituting the ingredients listed above. Let it rest for 20 minutes. Make the pastry cream by combining the eggs, egg yolks, sugar, orange juice and zest of 3 oranges. Beat until frothy.

Cream Pie

3. Soften the butter and add to the pastry cream. Bring this to a boil and beat well. Remove from heat, stir in the orange-flavored liqueur and let it cool. Refrigerate for 1 hour. Roll out the short pastry and fit it into a pie pan. Line it with wax paper and fill with dried beans. Bake for 15 minutes at 390 °F/200 °C. Remove the wax paper and the beans and bake for another 15 minutes.

4. Slice the orange and boil it in the syrup for 30 minutes. Brush the crust with guava jelly and place the sponge layer inside. Cover it with pastry cream and garnish the top with the candied orange slices.

Coconut

For the short pastry:
(see basic recipe)
2 cups/250 g flour
½ cup/125 g butter
1 egg
1 tbsp water
1 vanilla bean
2 tbsp/30 g sugar

Sponge cake: (see basic recipe)

For the filling:
7 oz/200 g plum of Cythere
6½ tbsp/100 ml coconut liqueur
a few tablespoons of water
5 eggs
3 egg yolks
1 cup/250 g brown sugar
3 pinches of cardamom
¾ cup plus 1 tbsp/75 g grated coconut
1 cup plus 5 tbsp/275 g butter

For the garnish:
2 tbsp/20 g candied fruit

Serves	4
Preparation time:	1 hour
Cooking time:	30 minutes
Chilling time:	30 minutes
Difficulty:	★

Plum of Cythere, a relative of the mango, is a very flavorful fruit with thin, yellow skin. When peeling this fruit, the skin comes off with a surprising amount of the pulp. This is not unusual and is, in fact, convenient because the outer flesh of this plum is very bitter. The pit has little thorns, just like a miniature sea urchin. Pitting these plums is always more time consuming than expected so one should be sure to plan enough time.

When the pulp is stirred it will release a delicious juice. If the juice is too thick, some water should be added. This extra water will help when straining the juice from the pulp.

Plum of Cythere may not be available in most markets in North America, but fortunately this pie is very accomodating of substitutions. Either pineapple or pomelo can be used as a base for the cream, following the same directions as for the plums. To simplify this recipe even further, canned juice may be used.

The coconut-plum mixture should be beaten well to prevent the eggs from coagulating. If this mixture is too thin, cornstarch or a little flour can be added. The sponge cake is literally being used as a sponge to absorb the excess juice. This absorbent quality will be enhanced if the sponge cake is made a day in advance. It will also be easier to slice the sponge.

A garnish of fresh or candied fruits in contrasting colors will give this pie an artistic flair.

1. Prepare the short pastry as described in the basic recipe but substituting the ingredients listed above. Roll it out and fit it into a pan. Bake it twice at 390 °F/200 °C for 15 minutes each time. Make the sponge cake as directed in the basic recipe. Slice a ¼ in/4 mm layer and place it in the pie crust. Pit the plums and strain them, reserving the juice.

2. Combine the coconut liqueur and water and brush this onto the sponge cake. Toast the grated coconut. In a large pot, combine the eggs, egg yolks, sugar, plum juice, cardamom and toasted coconut. Whip this mixture over low heat. Stir in the butter and bring to a boil.

Cream Pie

3. Let the cream cool in the refrigerator for about 30 minutes, then spread it over the sponge cake. Save a little for the garnish.

4. Using a pastry bag, garnish the pie with the pastry cream, then sprinkle a little coconut over it. Add some candied fruit, red currants or even a slice of candied orange.

Asian Pear

For the filling:
1 lime
1¼ cups/300 ml sweet white wine
½ cup/150 g honey
2 pinches of cinnamon
4 cloves
4 eggs
2 large Asian pears

For the sweet short pastry:
(see basic recipe)
1⅔ cups/200 g flour
6½ tbsp/100 g sugar
6½ tbsp/100 g butter
2 eggs

For the garnish:
¼ cup/50 g guava jelly
slivered almonds
fresh mint

Serves	6
Preparation time:	40 minutes
Resting time:	30 minutes
Cooking time:	55 minutes
Difficulty:	★

This tart is traditionally made with apples rather than Asian pears, but these pears give a truly unique and surprising flavor to this delicious recipe. Asian pears are increasingly available in regular supermarkets.

Asian pear trees withstand cold weather well and the fruit does not spoil as quickly as its more delicate cousin, the pear.

Sweet short pastry is fragile and should be handled very gently. A clever way to fit the crust into the pan without damaging it it to roll the pastry onto a rolling pin and then unroll it into the tart pan.

The pastry cream used here is wine-based. The spices are the traditional flavors of winter baking, sweet, spicy, and nostalgic.

They compliment the flavor of Asian pear perfectly and make this warm tart a true delicacy.

The addition of warm wine to the eggs will cause the eggs to develop a mousse-like consistency quickly. The tart is often briefly baked with the filling to prevent the pear slices from "drowning" in the filling. However, this step may be omitted. The slices can be laid out on the bottom of the crust and immediately covered with the filling. They should be baked for 30 minutes at 355 °F/180 °C.

The tart is done! All it needs, according to our chef, is a few leaves of fresh mint for garnish.

1. Peel the lime and julienne the zest. Pour the wine in a large pot and add the honey, cinnamon and crushed cloves. Bring to a boil for 5 minutes, then strain through a fine sieve. Prepare the sweet short pastry and let it rest for 30 minutes. Roll it out and fit it into a tart pan. Bake it twice for 10 minutes at 390 °F/200 °C.

2. Whisk the eggs and pour in the warm spiced wine while beating. Continue beating until the mixture has cooled completely. Spread the filling onto the pastry crust and bake for 10 minutes at 355 °F/180 °C.

Tart

3. Peel, seed and slice the Asian pears.

4. Arrange the slices on the filling in a spiral. Bake at 355 °F/180 °C for 20 minutes. Lightly toast the almonds. Using a little guava jelly, brush the edge of the pie crust and arrange the almonds along the edge. Garnish with fresh mint and serve warm.

10 fresh figs
6½ tbsp/100 g sugar
3½ tbsp/50 g butter
1 vanilla bean
2 tbsp/30 g mango jelly

For the sweet short pastry:
(see basic recipe)
3⅓ cups/400 g flour
13 tbsp/200 g butter
½ cup/60 g confectioners' sugar
1 egg
a pinch of salt
zest of ½ orange
zest of ½ lemon

For the caramel filling:
2 tbsp/30 g sugar
a few tsp of water
½ cup/125 ml milk
1 tbsp butter
1 egg
3½ tbsp/50 ml aged rum
2 tbsp/15 g flour

Serves   *6*
Preparation time: *35 minutes*
Cooking time: *40 minutes*
Difficulty: *★*

Most figs are grown in the Orient, and they are very popular in Mediterranean countries. Figs can be eaten fresh or dried and were a very important food source during biblical times. Phoenicians ate figs on their many long trips at sea, and thus unintentionally played a role in the distribution of figs to the rest of the world.

For this recipe, firm, smooth figs should be chosen. White or red ones are acceptable, though the red ones will look more attractive on the caramel.

The tart can be glazed with mango jelly, or even with guava or fig jelly. The glaze will give the tart extra shine and illuminate its finer qualities. Pears or mangoes may replace the figs in this dessert, and cinnamon or powdered licorice make intriguing substitutes for the vanilla.

An alternative way to prepare the figs is to simply cut them in half and sprinkle the inside with a mixture of sugar and finely ground almonds, and then broil them. With this method, the figs should be arranged sliced side up.

One attractive way to garnish this pie is to form a flower out of sliced fruit, as our chef has demonstrated with strawberries.

1. Cut the figs in half and place them in a pan with the sugar, butter and vanilla. Bake for 8–10 minutes at 460 °F/240 °C. Broil for the last 2 minutes to caramelize the figs. Set them aside on a plate.

2. Prepare the sweet short pastry as described in the basic recipe but substituting the ingredients listed above. Add the orange and lemon zest and let the dough rest for 20 minutes. Roll it out and fit it into a pan. Bake twice for 10 minutes each time. For the filling, make a caramel with the sugar and a little water. When the sugar has begun to turn golden brown, stir in the milk and butter.

Fresh Fig Tart

3. Remove the caramel from the heat and beat in the egg, rum and flour.

4. Pour the caramel into the tart shell and bake for 10 minutes at 355 °F/180 °C. Neatly arrange the figs on the caramel. Glaze the figs and filling with some warm mango jelly. If desired, use strawberry slices to garnish the pie.

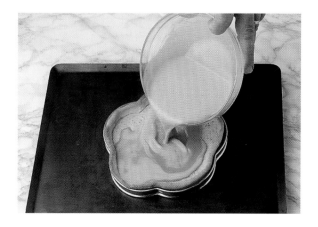

Chocolate

¾ cup/150 g candied kumquats

For the sweet short pastry:
(see basic recipe)
5 tbsp/75 g butter
¼ cup/60 g sugar
3 egg whites
2 cups/250 g flour
pinch of salt
¾ cup plus 1 tbsp/75 g grated coconut

For the chocolate filling:
12¼ oz/350 g dark chocolate
2 cups/500 ml heavy cream

For the garnish:
3½ oz/100 g dark chocolate

Serves	*6*
Preparation time:	*45 minutes*
Cooking time:	*20 minutes*
Chilling time:	*2 hours*
Difficulty:	★

This tart is a breeze to prepare, with a simple pastry and a foolproof chocolate filling. For a variation, milk chocolate can be substituted for the dark chocolate. For a completely different effect, white chocolate can be used.

Chocolate lovers can increase the amount of chocolate to their hearts' content.

The success of this tart depends largely on the quality of the chocolate, so it should be chosen with care. In general, the higher the cocoa content the better the chocolate. Other factors including the roasting process and the grinding of the beans. Good chocolate can be recognized by its brown, glossy color and by its consistency, which should be firm. A few curls of the chocolate should be shaved off and reserved for the garnish.

Kumquats are sometimes called *oranges naines*, or "dwarf oranges," and will add a delicate tang to the tart. They can be replaced by candied orange zest, which should be marinated in a little rum.

Chocolate Kumquat Tart should be made the same day it is served and should not be frozen, since the chocolate would develop white streaks which ruin its appearance, although they do not affect the flavor.

1. Prepare the sweet short pastry as described in the basic recipe but using the ingredients listed above. Let it rest for 30 minutes.

2. Roll out the pastry and fit it into a tart pan. Prick it with a fork to prevent it from rising too much as it bakes. Bake twice for 10 minutes each time. Breaking the chocolate for the filling into small pieces.

Kumquat Tart

3. Bring the cream to a boil and add the chocolate. Stir until the chocolate has completely melted. Let cool.

4. Slice the kumquats. Spread them out on the bottom of the crust. Pour the chocolate mixture into the crust and refrigerate for 2 hours. Garnish before serving.

Chocolate

1 lb/500 g mandarin oranges

For the filling:
4½ oz/125 g dark chocolate
½ cup/125 g butter
6½ tbsp/50 g powdered cocoa
4 eggs
6½ tbsp/100 g sugar

For the short pastry:
(see basic recipe)
1⅗ cups/200 g flour
½ cup/120 g butter
1 egg
1 tsp vanilla sugar
a pinch of salt
3½ tbsp/50 g sugar

Serves	*6*
Preparation time:	*20 minutes*
Cooking time:	*35 minutes*
Chilling time:	*30 minutes*
Difficulty:	*★*

Happy Easter! This springtime holiday is filled with happiness and joy. To express their joy, many chose to "say it with chocolate." Chocolate remains one of the most common Easter treats, whether in the form of Easter candies so popular with children or an elaborate chocolate pastry.

What a wonderful combination of flavors and colors chocolate and mandarin oranges make! This Caribbean fruit, as well as its zest, is often used in liqueurs.

Mandarin orange peel, which can remain green even when it is perfectly ripe, does not adhere to the pulp and is very easy to remove. However, the little white pieces of skin should be removed. Some segments should be set aside for the garnish and they can either be peeled or sliced directly from the orange, depending on how much time is available. The vanilla sugar used here replaces the vanilla bean often used in short pastries. The pastry should be fitted into the pan, but allow the dough to hang over the edges. Rolling over the pie pan with a rolling pin, will cut off the excess dough very neatly.

Our chef recommends a bittersweet chocolate to balance out the delicate tartness of the mandarin oranges. When adding the chocolate, it should be sprinkled evenly to avoid lumping.

This pie will surely convince your guests of your formidable talents in the kitchen!

1. For the filling, melt the chocolate in a double boiler. Combine the butter, melted chocolate, and cocoa. Separately, beat the eggs and the sugar until frothy, and then stir them into the chocolate mixture. Beat well until all the ingredients are thoroughly combined.

2. Prepare the short pastry as described in the basic recipe but substituting the ingredients listed above. Let it rest for 30 minutes. Bake it twice at 390 °F/200 °C for 15 minutes each time. Fill the pie crust with the chocolate filling and refrigerate for 30 minutes.

Mandarin Pie

3. Peel the mandarin oranges and remove all the bits of white skin.

4. Arrange the mandarin orange sections on the filling and serve.

Candied Pink

For the pastry cream:
(see basic recipe)
1 cup/250 ml milk
2 vanilla beans
7½ tbsp/110 g sugar
8 tsp/20 g flour
4 tsp/10 g cornstarch
2 eggs

For the Chiboust cream:
juice of ½ grapefruit
2 egg whites
3½ tbsp/50 g sugar
a pinch of salt
¾ cup plus 1 tbsp/75 g grated coconut

For the candied grapefruit:
2 pink grapefruits
2 cups/500 ml water
1¼ cup/300 g sugar

For the egg-white pastry:
(see basic recipe)
3 egg whites
5 tbsp/75 g butter
¼ cup/60 g sugar
¾ cup plus 1 tbsp/75 g grated coconut
1¼ cups/150 g flour
a pinch of salt
1 lemon

Serves 6
Preparation time: 1 hour 30 minutes
Cooking time: 1 hour 15 minutes
Chilling time: 45 minutes
Difficulty: ★

The reknowned French pastry chef, Chiboust, created a classic dessert which he named "Saint Honoré" after the street where his bakery was located (and the patron saint of bakers). The filling for this fabulous creation is called Chiboust cream after the inventor of this classic of French *pâtisserie*.

When preparing the Chiboust cream, care must be taken to add the grapefruit juice just before boiling the cream. This will prevent it from curdling. It is also important to add the ingredients in the proper order.

Once the egg-white pastry is made, it should be rolled out, fit into the pan and pricked with a fork. The pastry should be firmly pressed into the pan so that it does not form unattractive bubbles while baking.

The primary characteristic of citrus fruits is their combination of sweet yet tart flavors. Citrus fruits are generally grown in warm, sunny regions. While they used to be luxury items, they are now easy to find, which is very convenient since they are so nutritious. In this recipe, grapefruit can be replaced by another citrus fruit such as lemon or orange.

To decorate this pie, etch designs on the top of the pastry cream with the tip of a knife.

1. Prepare the pastry cream as described in the basic recipe but substituting the ingredients listed above. Add the grapefruit juice and let this mixture simmer gently for 5 minutes over low heat. Separately, beat the egg whites with the sugar and salt. Fold the egg whites into the pastry cream to create a Chiboust cream.

2. For the candied grapefruit, slice the fruit and poach in a sugar syrup made from the sugar and water (see basic recipes) for 40 minutes (20 minutes covered and 20 minutes uncovered to allow some of the water to evaporate).

Grapefruit Pie

3. Drain the candied grapefruit slices on a cooling rack until they reach room temperature. Set 2 aside. Make the egg-white pastry as described in the basic recipe but using the ingredients above, and let it rest 30 minutes. Press it into a pie pan and bake twice for 15 minutes each time at 390 °F/200 °C. Arrange the candied slices on the pie shell.

4. Spoon the Chiboust cream over the grapefruit slices. Dice the peel from the reserved slices and use it to garnish the top of the pie. Refrigerate for 45 minutes. To brown the top of the pie, carefully broil for a few minutes before serving.

Rice Pudding

For the rice filling:
¼ cup/50 g white rice
1 cup/250 ml milk
½ vanilla bean
a pinch of cinnamon
8 tsp/40 g sugar
2 egg yolks
1½ oz/40 g pastry cream (see basic recipe)
2 egg whites

For the lightly leavened dough:
(see basic recipe)
1 tbsp/12 g compressed fresh yeast *
2 cups/250 g flour
4½ tbsp/65 ml milk
1 tsp/5 g salt
1 tbsp/15 g sugar
2 eggs
½ cup/125 g butter

For the garnish:
confectioners' sugar

Serves | 6
Preparation time: | 1 hour
Resting time: | 30 minutes
Cooking time: | 50 minutes
Difficulty: | ★

Any good quality, long grain white rice will do for this recipe, keeping in mind that flavored rice must be strictly avoided. Cooking rice can be tricky and our chef suggests either boiling it in a double boiler over low heat, or baking the milk and rice in the oven. The rice should not be too hot when adding the egg yolks, or they will cook. Once the yolks have been added, the mixture should be placed in the pie crust as quickly as possible or it will harden and be very difficult to spread.

The vanilla can be replaced by cinnamon or cloves. A few raisins can also be added, or even a few diced candied oranges, which will enhance the flavor of the rice pudding.

Once the pie is removed from the oven, it is ready to be decorated, using only a cooling rack and confectioners' sugar. Holding the cooling rack over the pie while sprinkling the sugar is an easy way to form an attractive pattern.

This pie is best eaten warm, but is still very good cold. It will be even better served with a rum-flavored custard.

* In hot climates and tropical regions active dry yeast should replace the compressed fresh yeast. Use half the amount normally called for.

1. Rinse the rice and boil it gently in the milk with the vanilla bean and cinnamon for 25 minutes. As the rice is cooking, make the lightly leavened dough by crumbling the yeast into the flour, and then adding the milk, salt, sugar, eggs and softened butter.

2. Stir the dough well and let it rest for 30 minutes in a cool place. Roll out the dough and fit it into a pan. Set aside. Stir the sugar into the rice while it is still warm. After it has cooled, stir in the egg yolks.

Pie

3. Prepare the pastry cream according to the basic recipe and fold it into the rice mixture.

4. Whip the egg whites and fold them into the rice mixture. Fill the pie crust with the filling and bake for 25 minutes at 445 °F/230 °C. Let cool and sprinkle with confectioners' sugar.

Banana

For the short pastry:
(see basic recipe)
1½ cups/180 g flour
⅓ cup/80 g butter
1 egg
1 tbsp water
2 tbsp/30 g sugar
a pinch of salt
1 tsp vanilla sugar

For the filling:
2 lb 3 oz/1 kg bananas
1 cup/250 g sugar
3½ tbsp/50 g butter

Serves	*6*
Preparation time:	*30 minutes*
Resting time:	*30 minutes*
Cooking time:	*25 minutes*
Difficulty:	★

When Fanny, one of the Tatin sisters, accidentally turned over a tart she was about to put it in the oven, she certainly did not intend to create one of the most famous tarts in the history of French *pâtisserie*. Yet, she had just made one of the most innovative steps in baking. Despite the great success of this pastry, she died in total poverty.

Our chef suggests that when making this tart, ripe, soft bananas should be used. Regular bananas should be used, rather than red bananas or baby bananas, because the consistency when baked is quite different. The slices should have a slightly oblong shape and be attractively arranged on the sugar. It is important to remember that the bottom of the tart will end up on the top when served. Before putting the tart in the oven, our chef suggests placing the pan over a flame for a few moments, which will start the caramelization process and allow for a more even color. If this were attempted in the oven, the caramel would brown but the bananas would not cook through.

Unmolding a tarte tatin is always a little tricky since it is done while the tart is still hot and the caramel is liquid. Be careful to avoid burns from the caramel or the steam.

If for some reason dinner is running late and the tart has cooled in the pan, simply hold it over a flame to melt the caramel and then unmold it.

1. Make a short pastry as described in the basic recipe but using the ingredients listed above. Let it rest for 30 minutes. Cut out a piece of dough the size of the pan and set it aside. Slice the bananas about ⅜ in/1 cm thick.

2. Butter a tart pan with a pastry brush and sprinkle in the sugar so it lines the pan about ⅜ in/1 cm thick.

Tarte Tatin

3. Carefully lie the bananas on the sugar. This should be done in several rings, starting from the outside and working your way in. Caramelize the sugar for 2–3 minutes over the stove as described. Cover the bananas with the pastry and bake at 430 °F/220 °C for 25 minutes.

4. Once the tart has been removed from the oven, cover it with a plate that is larger than the pan. Flip the tart over onto the plate in one quick motion. Some caramel may leak onto the plate. This pie can be eaten warm or cool.

Banana

5 tsp/25 g sugar
3 tbsp water
1 clove
pinch of coriander
pinch of pepper
3 tbsp honey
2 tbsp confectioners' sugar

For the shortbread:
(see basic recipe)
2 cups/250 g flour
¼ cup/60 g sugar
½ cup/125 g butter
a pinch of salt
1 egg

Serves	6
Preparation time:	45 minutes
Resting time:	1 hour
Cooking time:	30 minutes
Difficulty:	★ ★

For the filling:
3 bananas
3 egg yolks
1 vanilla bean
3½ tbsp/50 g sugar
juice of 1 lemon
3½ tbsp/50 ml heavy cream
3½ tbsp/50 ml rum

For the doughnut batter:
(see basic recipe)
6½ tbsp/100 g flour
¼ cup/60 ml beer
2 eggs, separated
½ tsp salt
4 tsp/20 ml oil

Legend has it that merchants traveling the Mediterranean would often stop at a Tunisian port called La Goulette so that the sailors could stop to eat these wonderful fried bananas, which were served with fresh figs. This dessert, which traveled around the world with the sailors, made its way to the Caribbean.

To organize the preparation of this recipe, which requires two different doughs, each with distinct resting times, our chef suggests making the doughnut batter one hour in advance. To prevent the bananas from absorbing too much oil, a large pan should be used. The bananas should not be dropped in the oil, but gently placed in the pan with a spatula. The doughnut batter is not sweetened since the natural sweetness of the fruit is enough. Other fruits, such as papaya or persimmon, can be used instead of bananas.

This tart should be served warm and will be improved by the addition of spiced honey, prepared as follows: In a small pot, combine the sugar, water, and crushed pepper, coriander and clove. Bring this to a boil and remove from heat. Let it steep until it has completely cooled. Strain it through a fine sieve to remove the spices, then stir the liquid into the honey. Bring to a boil once more. When serving, either top the tart with the spiced honey or serve the honey on the side.

1. Prepare the shortbread as directed in the basic recipe but substituting the ingredients listed above. Bake it twice for 10 minutes each time at 390 °F/200 °C. Slice the bananas and set aside. Blend the remaining ingredients for the filling together. Spread this mixture into the crust and bake it for 10 minutes at 390 °F/200 °C.

2. Make the doughnut batter by mounding the flour and making a well in it, and pouring the beer, egg yolks, salt and oil into the well. Stir well. Beat the egg whites until firm and fold them into the batter. Let the batter rest 1 hour.

Fritter Tart

3. Dip the banana slices in the batter and fry them in the oil until they are golden brown.

4. Arrange the fried bananas in the pie crust. Sprinkle with confectioners' sugar and serve warm. Serve with spiced honey.

Caramelized

3 guavas
6½ tbsp/100 g brown sugar

For the pastry cream:
(see basic recipe)
1 cup/250 ml milk
1 vanilla bean
¼ cup/60 g sugar
8 tsp/20 g flour
2 egg yolks

For the short pastry:
(see basic recipe)
1⅔ cups/200 g flour
6½ tbsp/100 g butter
1 egg
2 tbsp water
1 vanilla bean
a pinch of salt

For the garnish:
a few leaves of fresh mint

Serves   6
Preparation time: 1 hour
Cooking time: 1 hour
Chilling time: 1 hour 50 minutes
Difficulty: ★

Guava is native to Central America and the Caribbean, but is now grown in the warm climates of Africa, South America and India as well. Because guava is rich in vitamin C and has so few calories, it has become very popular. Ripe guava has yellow skin, and its flesh is very tender and flavorful. Once ripe, guava should be eaten fairly rapidly or it will spoil. One should always be very careful not to buy overripe guava.

It has been said that every part of a guava can be eaten, but our chef suggests peeling and seeding the guava before eating it. Papaya or persimmon can be substituted if desired.

After baking the crust at 390 °F/200 °C, the oven should be allowed to cool down to 250 °F/120 °C before baking the fruit. Otherwise the outside of the fruit will burn and the inside will be undercooked.

To keep the guavas crunchy, a little sugar can be sprinkled over the tart before serving. Then the tart should be broiled for a few minutes. The color and texture of these caramelized guavas will be superb.

Adding cinnamon will spice up the pastry cream, and fresh mint leaves can be used to decorate the tart.

1. Prepare the pastry cream as described in the basic recipe, but substituting the ingredients listed above. Let it cool for 20 minutes.

2. Prepare the short pastry as described in the basic recipe but using the ingredients listed above. Let it rest for 30 minutes. Roll out the pastry and prick it with a fork before baking it twice at 390 °F/200 °C, for 15 minutes each time. Fill the baked crust with the pastry cream while it is still warm.

Guava Tart

3. Peel and seed the guavas. Slice them lengthwise and cover them thoroughly with brown sugar.

4. Arrange the guavas on the pastry cream to form an attractive flower shape. Bake at 250 °F/120 °C for 30 minutes and then broil to caramelize (see text). Let the tart cool for 1½ hours before serving.

Kumquat and

7 oz/200 g kumquats
3 cups water
1⅔ cups/400 g sugar
1⅔ cups/200 g flour
¾ cup plus 1 tbsp/200 g butter
6 eggs
1 tbsp orange-flower water
½ cup plus 1 tbsp/100 g finely ground hazelnuts

zest of 1 lime
1 tbsp whole hazelnuts
1 tbsp confectioners' sugar

Serves	6
Preparation time:	50 minutes
Cooking time:	1 hour
Difficulty:	★

Kumquats were originally cultivated in China, but are now found in the Far East, Australia and the United States. Kumquats are available year round.

About the size of a quail's egg, kumquats hide a deliciously tart pulp, rich in vitamin A, under a sweet yellow or orange skin. For this dessert firm, smooth fruit should be used. Also, the heavier the kumquats are, the more juice they contain. Blanching them will decrease their bitterness, and preserving them

softens their flavor. They will also develop a hint of orange flavor from the orange-flower water. The flavor of the lime zest is the perfect match for the hazelnuts. Other nuts or dried fruit may be substituted for the hazelnuts, if desired.

The kumquats should be arranged with their rounded side facing upward. A few pieces of chopped hazelnuts will complete the garnish.

1. Blanch the kumquats, then place them in a saucepan with the water and half the sugar. Simmer over low heat for 25 to 30 minutes.

2. In a separate pot, combine the flour and remaining sugar over low heat, without letting these ingredients cook. Melt the butter. Make a well in the center of the flour and sugar mixture and pour in the melted butter, eggs, orange-flower water and finely ground hazelnuts. Stir with a wooden spoon until a dough forms.

Hazelnut Pie

3. Grate 1–2 tsp of lime zest. Butter a 9 in/24 cm pie pan and press the dough made in Step 2 into it to form a crust. Bake for 30 minutes at 355 °F/180 °C. Unmold the pie crust and arrange the kumquats inside it.

4. Slice and lightly toast the whole hazelnuts. Sprinkle the confectioners' sugar and hazelnut pieces over the kumquats.
Cool and serve after adding a light sprinkling of lime zest.

Mango

For the short pastry:
(see basic recipe)
1⅔ cups/200 g flour
6½ tbsp/100 g butter
1 egg
2 tbsp water
a pinch of salt

For the mango filling:
1 lb/500 g mangoes
5 tsp/25 g sugar
5 tsp/25 g butter

For the almond cream:
¾ cup/200 ml whipping cream
¾ cup dark rum
2 egg yolks
5 tbsp/75 g sugar
3½ tbsp/25 g finely chopped almonds

For the garnish:
3½ tbsp/25 g slivered almonds

Serves | 6
Preparation time: | 1 hour 30 minutes
Cooking time: | 1 hour 5 minutes
Chilling time: | 1 hour
Difficulty: | ★ ★

Mangoes are available all year round. Between March and July mangoes are brought in from the Caribbean and the Ivory Coast, and the rest of the year they are imported from Brazil. There are many varieties of this exotic fruit, and it offers a multitude of culinary possibilities.

Mangoes have greenish skin on one side and are yellow, red or purple on the other. The red side has been exposed to the sun, and should be checked for ripeness. However, mangoes will continue to ripen at room temperature. It is best to buy firm fruit and wait for the perfect time to eat them: Cook them as soon as they are ripe—they are wonderful in curried dishes—or wait a few more days to use them in a dessert. The warm orange hue of the pulp is a wonderful decorative asset.

This tart has two novel features. Its shape is graceful and delicate, and the almonds add an unexpected touch. To make sure the slivered almonds stand up on the top of the tart without falling over or sinking, the cream should be allowed to set for about ten minutes before adding the almonds. To "moisture proof" the crust, it is advisable to brush it with some melted butter before it is filled.

The oven door should be kept closed while arranging the almonds so that the oven stays warm . The baking time for the almonds is very brief and they need to be watched closely so that they do not burn. This dessert should be served cool after a good meal.

1. Prepare the short pastry as directed in the basic recipe but substituting the ingredients listed above. Let it rest for 30 minutes. Roll out the pastry and fit it into a pan. Bake twice for 10 minutes each time. For the mango filling, peel and dice the mangoes, reserving 1 mango for the garnish. Lightly sauté the diced fruit with the sugar and butter over low heat for 20–25 minutes.

2. Let the mango compote cool, and refrigerate it for 30 minutes before spooning it into the crust. Slice half of the reserved mango and arrange the slices on the filling.

Almond Tart

3. Combine all the ingredients for the almond cream.

4. Cover the mangoes with the almond cream. Bake for 10 minutes at 390 °F/200 °C. Remove the tart from the oven and insert the slivered almonds upright in the filling. Bake another 10 minutes at the same temperature. Refrigerate for 30 minutes before serving.

Pepino and

For the filling:
1 lb/500 g pepinos
juice of 1 lime
2 cups/500 g brown sugar
¼ cup/30 g slivered almonds

For the sweet short pastry:
(see basic recipe)
1⅔ cups/200 g flour
6½ tbsp/100 g sugar
6½ tbsp/100 g butter
2 eggs

For the almond cream:
2 eggs
6½ tbsp/100 g sugar
¼ cup/30 g finely chopped almonds
a pinch of combava zest
¾ cup/200 ml whipping cream

Serves	*6*
Preparation time:	*40 minutes*
Cooking time:	*40 minutes*
Difficulty:	*★*

Pepinos are currently imported from New Zealand and Chili, though they originated in Peru. When ripe, its skin is yellow and striped. Its sweet, juicy pulp is very refreshing, with a flavor similar to melon and pear, though more subtle than either of those fruits. Pepinos are best when eaten cool. They should be peeled and seeded, then sprinkled with brown sugar or lemon juice; or a pinch of ginger and a little sugar sprinkled on them is a nice variation. They can also be served in a fruit salad or made into a sorbet.

Because pepinos are somewhat bland, our chef has chosen to liven this dessert up with the flavors of almonds, combava and lime. Combava is often used only for its zest and will keep in the refrigerator for two to three weeks. Women in Thailand boil combava and use the water as a hair conditioner. Because the combava flavor is very strong, it risks overwhelming the other ingredients and one must be careful to only use a little of the zest. Combava is not readily available in many parts of North America, but lime is a good substitute.

Brushing the crust with melted butter will "moisture proof" it and prevent the crust from becoming soggy. This pie should be baked at medium heat, like a quiche. The filling must not be allowed to boil, or the eggs and cream will separate and ruin its consistency. As long as it does not boil, the pie will have a smooth appearance which will mask any small air bubbles.

1. Peel, pit and slice the pepinos. Let the slices marinate in the lime juice and brown sugar. Prepare the sweet short pastry as directed in the basic recipe but substituting the ingredients listed above. Let it rest for 30 minutes. Roll out the pastry, fit it into a 9 in/22 cm pie pan, and bake it twice for 10 minutes each time.

2. To make the almond cream, beat the eggs with the sugar and then add the almonds, combava zest and whipping cream. Beat well and set aside.

Combava Pie

3. Drain the pepino slices and arrange them on the crust.

4. Pour the almond cream over the pepinos and sprinkle a few slivered almonds over it. Bake at 340 °F/170 °C for 20 minutes. Serve the pie warm.

Tamarind and

For the tamarind juice:
5¼ oz/150 g tamarind
1 cup/250 ml water
8 tsp/20 g cornstarch

For the sweet short pastry:
(see basic recipe)
1⅔ cups/200 g flour
6½ tbsp/100 g butter
6½ tbsp/100 g sugar
2 eggs
a pinch of salt

For the filling:
2 large, ripe bananas
1 cup/250 ml heavy cream
1 tsp cinnamon
3 egg yolks
⅓ cup/80 g sugar
2 tbsp/30 g brown sugar

Serves — *6*
Preparation time: — *1 hour 15 minutes*
Cooking time: — *50 minutes*
Chilling time: — *50 minutes*
Difficulty: — ★

Tamarind, also known as the Indian date, is a brown fruit which looks like a fat string bean. Its thick, swollen pod protects a sticky pulp. Tamarind is a popular snack food in the Caribbean; once peeled the fruit is dipped in sugar and eaten as a crunchy treat. Some even make a drink out of tamarind by letting the fruit soak in water overnight. It is then strained to remove the seeds and water is added to taste.

Canned tamarind juice may be substituted to save time. Because the tamarind juice will make the crust soggy, the crust must be brushed with melted butter to make it resistant to moisture before adding the juice. Once the juice is added, bake the pie for five minutes to allow the juice to set before the banana cream is added.

Ripe bananas should be used in this recipe to guarantee a tender filling. A variety of spices can be used to liven up the banana cream, such as cinnamon, nutmeg or vanilla, or even stronger flavors such as ginger or cloves. Bananas also go very well with rum.

Broil this pie just before serving, in the manner of a crème brûlée, to give the top that characteristic crunch.

1. Make the tamarind juice by first peeling and pitting the tamarinds. Soak them in warm water overnight. Remove any extra pieces of skin which may float to the surface.

2. Prepare the sweet short pastry as described in the basic recipe but using the ingredients listed above. Let it rest for 30 minutes. Roll out the pastry, prick it with a fork and fit it into a pie pan. Bake the crust twice, for 10 minutes each time, at 390 °F/200 °C. Brush it with melted butter. Whisk the cornstarch into the tamarind juice. Pour this mixture into the crust and bake for 5 minutes at 390 °F/200 °C.

Banana Brulée

3. For the filling, mash the bananas and beat in the cream, cinnamon, egg yolks and sugar. Stir briskly until well-mixed.

4. Carefully pour the filling into the crust and bake for 25 minutes at 275 °F/140 °C. Sprinkle the brown sugar on the top of the pie and broil for a few minutes to caramelize the surface. Refrigerate 50–60 minutes before serving.

2 tbsp/30 g guava jelly

For the egg-white pastry:
(see basic recipe)
5 tbsp/75 g butter
3 egg whites
1¼ cups/150 g flour
½ cup plus 1 tbsp/50 g grated coconut
¼ cup/60 g sugar
a pinch of salt
1 lemon

For the filling:
6½ tbsp/100 g sugar
½ tsp cinnamon
⅓ cup/50 g walnuts
½ cup plus 1 tbsp/50 g grated coconut
1 cup/250 ml heavy cream
1 egg yolk
10 walnuts, halved

Serves	*6*
Preparation time:	*40 minutes*
Cooking time:	*45 minutes*
Chilling time:	*1 hour*
Difficulty:	★ ★

Many myths about walnuts have sprung up over the centuries. For instance, it was once believed that walnuts cured headaches. Today, their flavor and nutritional attributes are the walnut's main selling points, whether they are served as a snack, as an ingredient in a mixed salad or even as a part of a stuffing or sauce. Dried walnuts are most often used in pastry-making. Fresh walnuts are harder to use because their bitter skin must be removed completely before eating them.

In this recipe, pecans can also be used. The slightly different shape of the nut gives this tart a distinctive look which will make it all the more appetizing. Our chef has made this tart more unique by using an egg-white pastry, but a simple short pastry or shortbread can be used just as easily. Because egg-white pastry is so fragile, care must be taken not to rip it as it is being placed in the pan. To facilitate the positioning of the pastry, it should be rolled onto a rolling pin and unrolled into the buttered tart pan. This will spread out its weight and keep it from tearing. Our chef suggests serving the tart in its pan due to the fragility of the crust.

This dessert is fairly easy to prepare and will certainly be a hit at a picnic or small gathering.

1. Prepare the egg-white pastry as described in the basic recipe but substituting the ingredients listed above. Let it rest for 30 minutes.

2. For the filling, combine the sugar, cinnamon, nuts and grated coconut. Stir this mixture into the cream. Continue to combine while adding the egg yolk.

Walnut Tart

3. Roll out the egg-white pastry and prick it with a fork. Fit the pastry into a pan, line it with foil and weigh it down with dried beans. Bake it for 10 minutes at 390 °F/200 °C. Remove the beans and the foil and bake the shell for another 10 minutes. Let the crust cool.

4. Pour the filling into the crust. Bake for 25 minutes at 390 °F/200 °C. Once cooled, decorate with the walnut halves and glaze the tart with slightly warmed guava jelly. Refrigerate for 1 hour before serving.

Lemon and

For the filling:
3 limes
3 lemons
13 tbsp/200 g butter
5 eggs
1 cup/250 g sugar
6½ tbsp/100 ml rum

For the short pastry:
(see basic recipe)
2 cups/250 g flour
½ cup/125 g butter
1 cup/125 g confectioners' sugar
a pinch of salt

For the garnish:
1 strawberry
1 lime
4 tsp sugar

Serves	*6*
Preparation time:	*25 minutes*
Cooking time:	*35 minutes*
Chilling time:	*30 minutes*
Difficulty:	*★*

While lemons and lime are similar in many respects, there are also several differences between them, including their color, size and the thickness of their skin. One way to choose juicy lemons and limes is by their weight. The heavier the fruit, the more juice it contains.

Limes are much more frequently used in the cuisine of tropical countries. They keep well stored in an air-tight container filled with sugar. The sugar will pick up the flavor of the lime and is a wonderful treat used in creams or even to flavor milk or tea.

Because the lemons and limes are not peeled in this recipe, they should be carefully washed beforehand.

The sugar and citrus combination gives this pie its sweet and sour character. This simple recipe is very flexible, and the lemons and limes can be replaced by other citrus fruit such as grapefruit, pomelo, clementines or oranges. The procedure remains the same with all these fruits, except the quantity of sugar should be reduced by 3½ tbsp/50 g. Any of these fruits will give the same contrast as the lemon/lime combination, but much less intensely.

Since this pie has such a light consistency, it is particularly welcome after a heavier meal.

1. Slice the limes and lemons without peeling them. Remove the seeds. Prepare a short pastry as described in the basic recipe but substituting the ingredients listed above. Let it rest for 20 minutes. Roll out the pastry, fit it into a pan and prick it with a fork. Bake it twice for 10 minutes and let it cool.

2. Purée the lemon and lime slices.

Lime Pie

3. Dice the butter. Heat it gently in a pan with the eggs, sugar and rum. Stir in the purée. Let simmer while stirring constantly for about 15 minutes.

4. Pour the filling into the crust and refrigerate for 30 minutes. Sprinkle sugar on the top and broil for a few minutes to create a thin caramel coating. Slice the strawberry. Peel the lime with a paring knife and make a rose shape with the zest. Garnish the pie with the strawberry slices and rosette.

Papaya

For the short pastry:
(see basic recipe)
1 cup/120 g flour
1 egg
3½ tbsp/50 g sugar
¼ cup/60 g butter
a pinch of salt

For the filling:
7 oz/200 g fromage blanc
1 tsp vanilla sugar
⅓ cup/80 g sugar
3 eggs, separated
7 oz/200 g papayas

Serves	*4*
Preparation time:	*35 minutes*
Resting time:	*30 minutes*
Cooking time:	*55 minutes*
Difficulty:	*★*

Cheese is an ancient and greatly valued food. Its origins are described in the Bible, in which bread and cheese are mentioned as a welcome gift.

Fromage blanc is a very soft and fresh cream cheese with a mild flavor. It is high in calories and in protein, though it is much easier to digest than the protein found in milk. It should be kept in the bottom of the refrigerator, where it is coldest. It is often eaten as a dessert with a little sugar or fruit, but it can also be used as an ingredient in dessert recipes, pies, soufflés or ice cream.

In this recipe, the vanilla can be replaced with orange-flower water and the cinnamon can be replaced with cloves. When ripe, papaya is served as an appetizer like melon, or as a dessert accompanied with cream. Our chef combines these uses in this pie. Papaya can be livened up with a little rum, or you could use mangoes instead. It is important to brush some melted butter on the crust to prevent it from becoming soggy.

This wonderful dessert is sure to be enjoyed by the whole family, and a good brut champagne is the perfect wine to accompany it.

1. Prepare the short pastry as described in the basic recipe but substituting the ingredients listed above. Let it rest for 30 minutes, then roll it out and fit it into the bottom of a pie pan. Bake it twice, for 15 minutes each time, at 355 °F/180 °C. Combine the fromage blanc with the vanilla sugar and sugar. Continue to blend until the sugar has completely dissolved.

2. Stir in the egg yolks.

Cheesecake

3. Peel and seed the papayas. Dice them and set aside a few pieces for the garnish. Stir the diced fruit into the cheese mixture.

4. Beat the egg whites until very firm and fold them into the papaya and cheese mixture. Pour the filling into the crust and decorate with the extra pieces of papaya. Bake for 25 minutes at 340 °F/170 °C. Let cool before unmolding.

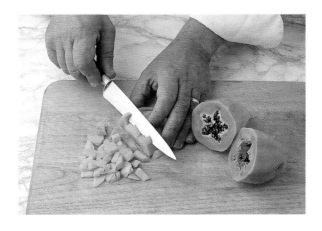

Banana Cream Pie

For the filling:
3 bananas
1 lime
¼ cup/30 g confectioners' sugar
1 large slice of watermelon
6½ tbsp/100 ml grenadine

For the short pastry:
(see basic recipe)
2 cups/250 g flour

½ cup/125 g butter
1 egg
2–3 tbsp water
1 vanilla bean
a pinch of salt

For the garnish:
a few green pistachios
1 carambola

Serves	*6*
Preparation time:	*35 minutes*
Cooking time:	*20 minutes*
Chilling time:	*15 minutes*
Difficulty:	*★*

Watermelon, which can be either oval or round, has a very refreshing flesh and its sweet, summery taste is delicious. Despite these qualities, watermelon has almost no nutritional value. The large black seeds found in watermelon, when dried and salted, go very well with cocktails such as anisette, ouzo or boukha (fig alcohol).

A good watermelon should be heavy and will not sound hollow when tapped. Plain sliced watermelon makes a great snack. It is excellent in fruit salad and when hollowed, becomes an eye-catching container for the fruit salad. To make watermelon jam, cook 2 lb 3 oz/1kg of watermelon with 3 cups of sugar. In certain countries, watermelon is harvested while it is still unripe and prepared like squash.

For the filling, only ripe bananas should be chosen since their flesh will be softer and more flavorful than firm bananas. Lime juice prevents the bananas from turning brown after they are peeled.

If you choose to garnish the pie with banana, it should be firmer than those used in the filling. It should also be sprinkled in lemon or lime juice to keep it from turning brown.

Other fruit such as melon, papaya or mango may be used depending on what is available and the preference of the chef.

1. Peel 2 of the bananas for the filling and purée them in a food processor with the lime and confectioners' sugar.

2. Using a cookie cutter or paring knife, cut out petal-like shapes from a pitted slice of watermelon, about ⅜ in/1 cm thick. Prepare the shortbread as described in the basic recipe but substituting the ingredients listed above. Let it rest for 30 minutes, then roll it out and fit it into a pan. Bake twice for 10 minutes each time.

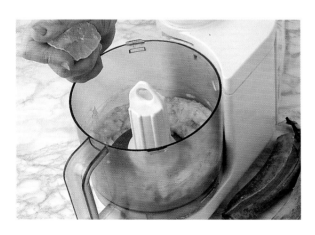

with Watermelon

3. Coat the watermelon petals in grenadine. Once the crust has cooled, fill it with the banana purée and arrange the petals on top of the filling.

4. Slice the remaining banana and insert the slices around the edge of the pie. Decorate the center with carambola or pistachio nuts. Refrigerate for 15 minutes before serving.

Nigella Seed and Orange-

½ cup/80 g rice
¾ cup/180 ml milk
a pinch of nigella seeds
6½ tbsp/100 g sugar
1 lemon
1 cup/250 ml whipping cream

For the sweet short pastry:
(see basic recipe)
1 cup/125 g flour
½ cup/125 g butter
1 egg
1 egg yolk
6½ tbsp/100 g sugar

For the custard:
(see basic recipe)
3 egg yolks
¼ cup/60 g sugar
1 cup/250 ml milk
2 sheets of gelatin
¾ cup water
1 tsp orange-flower water

For the garnish:
1 orange (optional)
a few pinches of nigella seeds
2 tbsp/30 g guava jelly

Serves — *6 to 8*
Preparation time: — *1 hour*
Cooking time: — *45 minutes*
Chilling time: — *2 hours*
Difficulty: — *★ ★*

Rice was one of the first cereals cultivated by mankind. It is now eaten world-wide after having been the staple of Asian diets for more than 3000 years. Today, rice is also an integral part of the cuisine of the south Caribbean.

When cooked with milk, rice becomes one of the bases for sweet flavored desserts. In this recipe, if time permits, it would be best to blanch the rice to remove its starch and then rinse it under cold, running water. The nigella seeds add a distinct flavor, which is mellowed by the orange-flower water. Nigella seeds are available in Indian and Middle Eastern groceries.

When prebaking or blind baking a crust, there are two important steps. During the first stage, which lasts ten to fifteen minutes, the crust should be covered with tin foil and weighted down with dried beans or baking weights. In the second step, which also lasts ten to fifteen minutes, the crust is baked without covering.

A tip from our chef: Gelatin sets quickly, so add the whipped cream before the custard mixture begins to set.

Nigella seeds make a distinctive garnish for this pie, along with orange zest sliced in the shape of half moons. The pie can also be glazed with warmed guava jelly to add extra shine. The contrast between the tangy lemon and the soft cream will thrill your guests.

1. Prepare the sweet short pastry as described in the basic recipe but using the ingredients listed above. Let it rest for 30 minutes, then roll it out and prebake twice, for 10 minutes each time, at 355 °F/180 °C. Boil the rice in milk with the nigella seeds. Peel and then dice the lemon. When the rice is half done, add the sugar and lemon zest. Stir the diced lemon into the cooked rice and let cool.

2. Make the custard by beating the egg yolks and sugar until pale and frothy. Bring the milk to a boil and pour it onto the egg yolks, stirring constantly, and let simmer until the custard thickens. Separately, dissolve the gelatin in the water and blend it in. Add the orange-flower water as well.

Flower Rice Pudding Pie

3. Whip the cream and fold it into the custard before it sets. Refrigerate for 1 hour.

4. Place a springform pan around the pastry and spread the rice filling on it, then pour in the custard. Garnish with nigella seeds and orange zest and refrigerate for at least 1 hour. Unmold and serve cold.

Piña Colada

Puff pastry: (see basic recipe)

For the filling:
1 small pineapple
1¼ cups/300 ml water
½ cup plus 2 tbsp/150 g sugar
1 egg yolk

For the pastry cream:
(see basic recipe)
1 cup/250 ml milk
¼ cup/60 g sugar

2 tbsp/15 g flour
4 tsp/10 g cornstarch
1 egg yolk
3½ tbsp/50 ml dark rum
3½ tbsp/50 ml coconut liqueur

For the garnish:
candied fruit
⅓ cup/100 g pineapple jelly

Serves	6
Preparation time:	1 hour
Cooking time:	50 minutes
Chilling time:	1 hour
Difficulty:	★

The coconut, king of trees! Its leaves form a royal crown atop its noble trunk, and since time immemorial, coconut has reigned supreme in Asian and Polynesian cuisine. Coconut is used in a vast variety of dishes. Marco Polo was the first European to discover and promote it, describing it as "sweet as sugar, white as milk, providing both food and drink."

In combination with pineapple and rum, coconut serves as a key element in that world-famous tropical drink, the piña colada. This delightful tart skillfully combines the same principal flavors into an intoxicating dessert. The pineapple must be chosen with care. It should be firm, heavy and have a strong aroma, and its stem or leaves should be bright green and shiny.

To prevent the pastry from rising unevenly as it bakes it should be pricked with a fork. Bake it carefully, because once the fruit and pastry cream are arranged it cannot be returned to the oven.

No time to make pastry cream from scratch? Is coconut liqueur missing from your liquor cabinet? No need to panic. Pastry cream can be purchased; 14 oz/400 g should be enough. One half cup/40 g of grated coconut can replace the liqueur. And for the glaze, the juice in which the pineapple cooks can be reduced and a little gelatin added.

Like a refreshing piña colada, this tart should be served cold.

1. Prepare the puff pastry as described in the basic recipe. Roll it out to about ⅛ in/3 mm thick. Make 4 strips about ½ in/1.5 cm wide as well as 1 large rectangle for the base of the tart. Brush an egg yolk over the rectangle and affix the thin strips on the edges. Decorate these strips with a the point of a knife if desired and brush them with more egg yolk. Bake for 20 minutes at 390 °F/200 °C.

2. Peel the pineapple and remove all the little black "eyes." Slice the pineapple and simmer the slices in the water and sugar for 30 minutes. Drain them on a cooling rack.

Tart

3. Prepare the pastry cream as described in the basic recipes but substituting the ingredients listed above. Blend in the rum and coconut liqueur. Fill the crust with the cream.

4. Carefully arrange the candied pineapple slices on the pastry cream. Garnish by inserting other candied fruits between the pineapple slices and finish by glazing with pineapple jelly. Refrigerate the tart for 1 hour before serving.

Banana Coconut

For the short pastry:
(see basic recipe)
1½ cups/180 g flour
⅓ cup/80 g butter
1 egg
1 tbsp water
2 tbsp/30 g sugar
a pinch of salt

Serves	6
Preparation time:	45 minutes
Cooking time:	42 minutes
Difficulty:	★

For the filling:
3 bananas
juice of 1 lemon
2 tbsp/30 ml dark rum
3½ tbsp/50 g butter, melted
a pinch of cinnamon
a pinch of nutmeg
1 clove
a pinch of ginger
¾ cup plus 1 tbsp/75 g grated coconut
3 drops of vanilla extract
6½ tbsp/100 ml honey
2 eggs
1 cup/250 g sugar

The spices used in this pie were once very rare and very expensive. When a whole barrel of cinnamon was set ablaze at a banquet in honor of Charles Quint (son of Philippe le Beau, Archduke of Austria and Jeanne Lafolle, Queen of Castilla), the 16th century nobility delighted at the extravagance.

In this recipe, the sweet, mild flavor of bananas melds with the spicy flavors of ginger and clove. Our chef has carefully chosen the perfect amount of each so that none overpowers the other. There are several different varieties of bananas. The small red bananas, which are superb for eating out of hand, are too firm to form a smooth purée and should not be selected for this dessert. Ordinary bananas should be used to yield a smooth purée and delicate slices. Saffron or curry can be substituted for the other spices for a surprising variation. Since curry includes ginger, cloves and nutmeg, these three flavors will predominate in this variation. Traditionally, candied ginger is used when making desserts. However, our chef recommends powdered ginger for this pie. When used conservatively, its distinctive flavor will enhance the sugar and the bananas without overshadowing the other spices.

It is vital to add the lemon juice as soon as the bananas are puréed so that they do not brown and spoil the dessert.

1. Prepare the short pastry as described in the basic recipe but substituting the ingredients listed above. Let it rest for 30 minutes, then roll out the pastry, prick it with a fork and fit it into a buttered tart pan.

2. Peel and mash 1 banana with a fork. Stir in the lemon juice, rum and melted butter. Add the spices, coconut, vanilla, honey, eggs and the sugar. Stir until all the ingredients are thoroughly combined.

Spice Pie

3. Peel and slice the 2 remaining bananas and arrange them in the pie crust. Save 6 of the nicest slices and sauté them in butter for 1–2 minutes. Use them to garnish the pie after it is baked.

4. Spoon the banana purée over the sliced bananas. Bake the pie on the middle rack of the oven for 10 to 15 minutes at 390 °F/200 °C and then for 20 to 25 minutes at 210 °F/100 °C. Let it cool before unmolding. Garnish and serve.

Louisiana

Sweet short pastry: (see basic recipe):

For the milk chocolate filling:
⅔ cup/100 g hazelnuts
2 cups/500 ml heavy cream
12¼ oz/350 g milk chocolate

For the white chocolate filling:
1 cup/250 ml heavy cream
5¼ oz/150 g white chocolate

For the dark chocolate filling:
1 cup/250 ml heavy cream
7 oz/200 g dark chocolate
½ cup/80 g candied orange zest

Serves	*6*
Preparation time:	*1 hour*
Cooking time:	*20 minutes*
Chilling time:	*3 hours*
Difficulty:	*★ ★*

This tart combines three different chocolates—dark, milk and white—into a most unique and memorable dessert. The colors of the chocolate give the tart an elegant look.

Our chef has dedicated this tart to to the people of Louisiana who have passed on Creole customs and traditions through many generations.

The sweet short pastry should be made as described in the basic recipe and then allowed to refrigerate overnight. It should be rolled out, pricked with a fork, then eased into a tart pan and baked for ten minutes at 390 °F/200 °C. This tart is filled in three steps. The instructions and times for freezing and cooling must be followed exactly to maintain the distinct separation between the fillings.

One possible variation, even tastier but less striking visually, is to substitute a coffee-flavored chocolate for the white chocolate. Small pieces of candied ginger can be added to spice up the dark chocolate; they will add zing to the whole tart.

Alcohol should not be added in any form, as it will prevent the chocolate from hardening.

The Louisiana Creole Tart should be removed from the refrigerator one hour before serving to allow the chocolate to soften to the proper consistency.

1. Make the sweet short pastry as described in the text. For the milk chocolate filling, coarsely crush the hazelnuts. Boil the cream. Break the milk chocolate into pieces and pour the boiling cream on it. Let this mixture cool and stir in the hazelnuts. Using a large round ring, pour the milk chocolate filling into the tart shell as indicated in the photo below. Freeze for 30 minutes.

2. Prepare the 2 other fillings in this manner. Using a smaller ring or biscuit cutter, fill the next area with the white chocolate and freeze for another 30 minutes.

Creole Tart

3. Dice the candied orange zest and gently stir it into the dark chocolate filling.

4. Fill the center of the tart with the dark chocolate filling and refrigerate for at least 2 hours. Let the tart sit at room temperature for 1 hour before serving.

Surprise

For the shortbread:
(see basic recipe)
2 cups/250 g flour
3½ tbsp/50 g sugar
½ cup/125 g butter
1 egg
a pinch of salt

For the filling:
⅓ cup/50 g raisins
3½ tbsp/50 ml orange-flavored liqueur
3 egg yolks
½ cup plus 2 tbsp/150 g sugar
1½ oz/40 g fresh ginger
zest and juice of 1 lemon
10 tbsp/150 g butter

For the meringue:
1 cup/250 g sugar
2 cups/500 ml water
5 egg whites
¼ cup/30 g pistachios
a pinch of salt

For the garnish:
⅓ cup/50 g pistachios

Serves	6
Preparation time:	1 hour
Cooking time:	55 minutes
Difficulty:	★ ★

The "surprise" of this tart is the combination of the powerful flavor of ginger with the very sweet meringue. The meringue is so sweet that you may be tempted to reduce the quantity of sugar called for. However, the meringue will not stiffen properly without using this amount, and the general appearance of the tart would suffer.

If this dessert seems just too sweet for your taste, the meringue can be replaced with plain whipped cream, whose consistency is not dependent on sugar. If you choose whipped cream, the final baking should be omitted, as the whipped cream would melt. This variation makes a tasty dessert, but lacks the succulent ginger-meringue combination and that delicious element of surprise.

The success of the sugar syrup relies on the proper cooking temperature of 250 °F/120 °C. It is best to use a candy thermometer to determine when the syrup has reached the correct temperature, but if no thermometer is available, cook the syrup until it forms large bubbles and reaches the "soft-ball" stage. This is when a small amount of syrup dripped from a spoon into ice cold water will form a small soft ball.

For variety, rum can be used instead of orange-flavored liqueur, and lime instead of lemon.

1. Prepare the shortbread as described in the basic recipe but substituting the ingredients listed above. Let it rest for 30 minutes. Roll it out and fit it into a form, cover with foil and weight it down with dried beans. Bake for 10 minutes at 390 °F/200 °C. Soak the raisins in the liqueur. Grate the ginger. Melt the butter. Separately, beat the egg yolks with the sugar until frothy.

2. While beating, add the ginger, lemon juice and zest, drained raisins and the melted butter. Fill the crust with this mixture and bake for 15 minutes at 355 °F/180 °C.

Meringue Tart

3. For the meringue, boil the sugar and water together for about 5 minutes until it reaches a temperature of 250 °F/120 °C. Beat the egg whites with a pinch of salt. Very slowly pour the sugar syrup onto the egg whites while continuing to beat until they have cooled completely. Chop the pistachios and fold them in.

4. Using a pastry bag with a star tip, decorate the tart with the meringue. Sprinkle some pistachios on the meringue and bake for 30 minutes at 320 °F/160 °C.

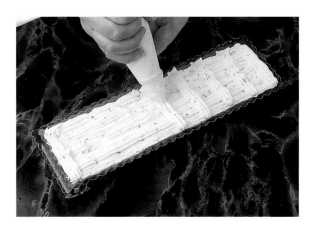

Coffee

For the shortbread:
(see basic recipe)
1⅔ cups/200 g flour
6½ tbsp/100 g butter
2 tbsp milk
3½ tbsp/50 g sugar
a pinch of salt

For the coffee filling:
2 tbsp instant coffee
3 tbsp water
8¾ oz/250 g cream cheese
1 tbsp crèmefraîche
½ cup plus 2 tbsp/150 g sugar
a pinch of salt
2 eggs
2 carambolas

For the coffee cream:
1 egg yolk
3½ tbsp/50 g butter
8 tsp/40 g sugar

For the garnish:
¼ cup/50 g mango jelly
a few coffee beans

Serves	*6*
Preparation time:	*2 hours*
Cooking time:	*40 minutes*
Chilling time:	*1 hour 30 minutes*
Difficulty:	★ ★

Coffee is one of the principal crops of many countries in Africa, South America and the Caribbean. There are two main types of coffee: arabica and robusta. Arabica is mellower and more flavorful than robusta, which is hardier and easier to grow. Arabica also contains less caffeine and is less bitter.

The origins of the carambola, the "star" of this recipe, are more obscure. One theory holds that a doctor/philosopher named Averroès was living in Marrakech, Morocco, when he discovered this fruit and named it "averrhoa carambola." India seems a likely origin for the carambola because of the commercial ties between India and Morocco at the time. The carambola is crisp, tart and flavorful and does not need to be peeled before eating. It cuts into lovely star-shaped slices, making it a good choice for garnishes. Its mild tartness will contrast well with the smooth flavor of the coffee.

Our chef recommends gently scraping the veins of the carambola if they have darkened, and also to avoid filling the pie with too much cream, or the carambola will sink.

This recipe has several steps and it is fairly time consuming, but the result will be well worth the effort.

1. Prepare the shortbread as directed in the basic recipe but substituting the ingredients listed above. Let it rest for 30 minutes, then roll it out and fit it into a tart pan. Bake the crust twice, for 10 minutes each time, at 430 °F/220 °C.

2. Dissolve the instant coffee in the water. Separately, whisk together the cream cheese, crème fraîche, sugar and salt. Whisk in the eggs and beat thoroughly. Pour in half of the dissolved coffee and stir well.

Carambola Pie

3. For the coffee cream, stir the egg yolk and sugar in a double boiler until the sugar has completely melted. Add the butter and remaining coffee. Refrigerate for 1½ hours.

4. Pour the cream cheese filling into the crust and bake for 20 minutes at 300 °F/150 °C. When it has cooled, spoon the coffee cream on top. Arrange the sliced carambola on the surface and glaze with some warm mango jelly. Garnish with a few coffee beans if desired.

Asian Pear

For the sweet short pastry:
(see basic recipe)
1⅔ cups/200 g flour
6½ tbsp/100 g sugar
6½ tbsp/100 g butter
2 eggs

For the marzipan:
2 egg yolks
½ cup/125 g sugar
1 cup/120 g flour
5 tbsp/50 g finely ground almonds

For the filling:
2 large Asian pears
⅓ cup/50 g pine nuts
3 tbsp/40 g mango jelly

Serves   *6*
Preparation time: *40 minutes*
Cooking time: *30 minutes*
Difficulty: ★

While this pie uses exotic and unusual ingredients, it is based on an old classic: apple pie. Though they resemble Golden Delicious apples, the flesh and flavor of Asian pears are more like pears. There are different varieties of this fruit, recognizable by the different skin colors. They range includes golden-brown, yellow-green, light yellow and golden. They are increasingly popular and are now often available in the tropical fruits section of supermarkets. Other names for this fruit include "apple pear" and "Japanese pear." When buying Asian pears, choose firm, smooth pears with no spots. This versatile fruit can be eaten in many forms: in an entree, side dish or a dessert.

Making marzipan can be tricky and our chef suggests combining the ground almonds with the flour before adding them to the wet ingredients to prevent lumping. The combination of pine nuts and almonds was a stroke of genius on the part of our chef. The small, oblong pine nut has a flavor similar to the almond's, but stronger and more resinous.

The peel from the Asian pears will make a charming garnish for this pie. It will not darken if soaked in water before use. The peel can be wound into the shape of a rose and placed on the pie just before baking. It can also be delicately tinted with food dye to make the rose even more realistic and add color to the pie.

1. Prepare the sweet short pastry as described in the basic recipe but substituting the ingredients listed above. Let it rest for 30 minutes, then roll it out and fit it into a pan. Bake the crust twice for 10 minutes each time at 355 °F/180 °C. In a large bowl, beat the egg yolks and sugar until pale and frothy.

2. Combine the flour and ground almonds. Gently stir this into the egg yolk mixture.

and Nut Pie

3. Peel and core the pears and slice them into even pieces with a sharp knife. Fill the crust with marzipan.

4. Artistically arrange the pear slices in a circle around the edge and in the middle. Sprinkle pine nuts over the pears. Bake for 10 minutes at 355 °F/180 °C. Do not let the pine nuts brown before the pears are done. Remove from the oven and glaze with a little mango jelly. Serve the pie warm.

Banana

For the shortbread:
(see basic recipe)
2 cups/250 g flour
6½ tbsp/100 g sugar
½ cup/125 g butter
3 tbsp water
a pinch of salt

For the banana filling:
3 ripe bananas
juice of 1 lemon
3 egg yolks
3½ tbsp/50 ml heavy cream
3½ tbsp/50 g brown sugar
6½ tbsp/100 ml dark rum
1 vanilla bean
3 firm bananas

Serves   *6*
Preparation time: *30 minutes*
Cooking time: *45 minutes*
Chilling time: *1 hour 30 minutes*
Difficulty: ★

The pattern of the banana slices decorating this pie resembles a daisy. The vanilla-flavored bananas are very tasty, though cinnamon can be used in place of the vanilla. Rum enhances all the other flavors.

Because the banana has such a smooth, mellow consistency, it assimilates spices very well. Even pepper or coriander can be added for a surprising and original twist.

Regular bananas are better suited for baking than the red or yellow dwarf varieties. Softer, riper bananas will work best for the filling, while the firmer bananas should be saved for the decorative topping.

Our chef recommends slicing the bananas at the last minute so that they do not darken. Also, the slices should be fairly thick so that if they begin to sink they will not be totally hidden. If the sugar does not caramelize sufficiently during baking, it can be broiled very briefly to finish off the process.

This pie is best served cold and should be prepared several hours in advance.

1. Prepare the shortbread as described in the basic recipe but substituting the ingredients listed above. Let it rest for 30 minutes, then roll it out and fit it into a buttered flan ring or springform pan. Bake it twice, for 10 minutes each time, at 390 °F/200 °C. In a large bowl, mash the ripe bananas with the lemon juice. Beat in the egg yolks, cream, brown sugar, rum and vanilla.

2. Once the crust has cooled, fill it with the banana mixture.

Rum Pie

3. Slice the remaining bananas. Arrange them on the filling in the shape of a flower.

4. Cover the bananas with additional brown sugar. Bake the pie for 25 minutes at 410 °F/210 °C to caramelize the sugar. Refrigerate for 1½ hours before serving.

Trinidad

For the rich shortbread:
1 egg
½ cup/125 g sugar
a pinch of salt
zest of 1 lemon
2 cups/250 g flour
2 tbsp water
½ cup/125 g butter

For the fruit topping:
3 mangoesteens
5 kiwi
1 tbsp guava jelly
a few cape gooseberries

For the pastry cream:
1 cup/250 ml milk
7½ tbsp/110 g sugar
8 tsp/20 g flour
4 tsp/10 g cornstarch
2 egg yolks

Serves	*6*
Preparation time:	*45 minutes*
Cooking time:	*30 minutes*
Chilling time:	*1 hour*
Difficulty:	★

Mangoesteens are troublesome to produce since the mangoesteen tree bears fruit only ten or fifteen years after being planted. Even trees grown from grafts require eight or nine years to bear fruit. Despite this, mangoesteens are common throughout the tropics. The fruit should be picked when ripe. Its skin is the color of red wine and about ⅜ in/1 cm thick, and its soft flesh has the color and consistency of litchis. The mangoesteen has one large pit like an avocado, but is divided into sections like an orange. Its tart, light flavor melts in the mouth.

The combination of mangoesteens, kiwi and cape gooseberries is delightful, and the varying levels of tartness combine in perfect harmony. The contrasting colors and shapes of the fruit make this dessert a work of art. This tart is also quite nutritious: The kiwi and cape gooseberry are rich in vitamin C and the cape gooseberry contains iron and phosphorus. Mangoesteen and cape gooseberry may be difficult to find in North American markets; the tart can be made with the kiwi alone, perhaps with strawberries replacing the more exotic tropical fruits.

A spatula will be a good utensil to work this dough, which should not be kneaded or it will toughen. Our chef suggests preparing the dough a day in advance so that it is more malleable. This tart is very simple to make and would be the perfect snack to have on hand when children come home from school.

1. In a large bowl, thoroughly combine the sugar and egg. Add the salt and a pinch of lemon zest. Sprinkle the flour over this mixture and pour in the water. Mix well. Place the dough on a work surface and add the softened butter. Stir the dough without kneading it until it forms a ball. Let the dough rest for 30 minutes, then roll it out, fit it into a tart pan and prick with a fork.

2. Cover the tart shell with aluminum foil and weigh it down with dried beans or baking weights. Bake the crust for 15 minutes at 390 °F/200 °C. Remove the aluminum foil and weights and bake it again for 15 minutes at the same temperature.

Tart

3. Peel the mangoesteens and separate into sections. Peel and slice the kiwi. Prepare the pastry cream as described in the basic recipe but substituting the ingredients listed above.

4. Spoon the cold pastry cream into the crust. Arrange the kiwi slices in a circular pattern on the pastry cream. Add the mangoesteen sections. Slice the cape gooseberries and arrange them in the middle of the tart. Glaze with guava jelly to add shine. Refrigerate for 1 hour before serving.

For the filling:
6 lemons
3½ tbsp/50 g butter
6 eggs
½ cup plus 2 tbsp/150 g sugar

For the shortbread:
(see basic recipe)
1⅔ cups/200 g flour
¼ cup/60 g sugar
6½ tbsp/100 g butter
3 tbsp water
a pinch of salt

For the garnish:
1 lemon
6½ tbsp/100 ml water
6½ tbsp/50 g confectioners' sugar

Serves — *6*
Preparation time: — *30 minutes*
Cooking time: — *1 hour 5 minutes*
Chilling time: — *40 minutes*
Difficulty: — ★

When making the filling for this pie, it is essential to stir the eggs constantly to prevent them from sticking to the pan. There are several tasty variations for this dessert. Limes will add an extra tang, using oranges or mandarin oranges will make the pie sweeter, and grapefruit will add a slightly bitter flavor. Pineapple can also be used, but in this case the filling should be flavored with lime zest and candied pineapple slices should be used for the garnish.

The lemon slices for the garnish should be candied by boiling them in a classic sugar syrup (see basic recipes) before beginning the rest of the recipe. This will save time and effort when the soufflé is finished.

The lemons or limes must be carefully cleaned before removing the zest. Also, the white layer under the peel should be removed, for it is very bitter. The success of a soufflé lies in the preparation of the egg whites. The stiffer the whites are, the more the soufflé will rise. A little confectioners' sugar can be sprinkled on the top of the pie towards the end of baking to form a thin, glossy layer of caramel.

1. Remove the zest from the lemons and slice it into julienne. Juice the lemons, and set aside. Melt the butter. Bring the lemon zest and lemon juice to a boil. Remove from heat, add the butter and set aside. Prepare the shortbread as described in the basic recipe but substituting the ingredients listed above. Let it rest for 30 minutes.

2. Roll out the shortbread and fit it into a pan. Bake it twice for 15 minutes each time. Separate the eggs and set the whites aside. Beat the yolks and sugar together in a pan until frothy. Reheat the lemon-butter mixture and when just boiling pour onto the egg yolks. Stir until mixture begins to boil, then let cool.

Soufflé Pie

3. Beat the egg whites until very stiff. Fold them into the cooled lemon cream.

4. Pour the lemon cream into the tart shell and bake for 5 minutes at 390 °F/200 °C. Do not allow the top of the pie to darken. Candy a few slices of lemon in sugar syrup (see basic recipe) for about 30 minutes. Drain them thoroughly and use to garnish the tart. Refrigerate for 40 minutes before serving.

Persimmon and Passion

4 ladyfingers
4 persimmons
2 tbsp butter
¼ cup/60 g sugar
4 passion fruits
2 tbsp crème fraîche
fresh mint leaves

For the short pastry:
(see basic recipe)
1 cup/120 g flour
1 egg
a pinch of salt
¼ cup/60 g butter
5 tsp/25 g sugar

Serves	*4*
Preparation time:	*20 minutes*
Cooking time:	*30 minutes*
Difficulty:	★

Persimmons are about the size of small tomatoes, and turn from light to bright orange as they ripen. Passion fruit grows on vines covered with thorns, which resemble hammers and nails.

The tart flavor of the passion fruit will go well with the milder taste of persimmon. Other possibilities our chef suggests for these tartlets are guava and lime or pear and lemon, both of which make delicious combinations. The ladyfinger crumbs sprinkled into the bottom of each tartlet are used to absorb the juice that the persimmons give off as they bake. Sponge cake or stale biscuits can substitute for the ladyfingers, but they should be crushed into small crumbs.

In this recipe, baking is done in two steps. The first baking, in a very hot oven (430 °F/220 °C), will prevent the tart shells from shrinking, while the second one, at 300 °F/150 °C, will bake the fruit without burning either the fruit or the crusts. One can tell if the persimmons are done by inserting a knife into the fruit. If the persimmons yield easily to the knife, they are done.

This dessert is a refreshing finish to a spicy or exotic meal.

1. Prepare a short pastry according to the basic recipe, but using the ingredients listed above. Roll it out and cut out 4 circles 4 in/10 cm in diameter. Fit each circle into a tart mold. Crush the ladyfingers with a rolling pin and sprinkle the crumbs on the bottom of each shell.

2. Remove the top of each persimmon and cut an "X" into that end. Insert a small piece of butter in each incision and very lightly sprinkle with sugar. Place 1 persimmon in each tartlet. Bake for 10 minutes at 430 °F/220 °C, and then for 20 minutes at 300 °F/150 °C.

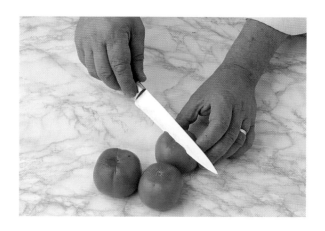

Fruit Cream Tartlets

3. Remove the seeds and pulp from the passion fruit and combine with the crème fraîche. Stir in the sugar and refrigerate.

4. Pour a spoonful of passion fruit cream over each tartlet. Serve warm with a little chopped fresh mint, if desired.

Blancmange

For the almond milk:
3 cups/500 g crushed almonds
1 cup/250 g sugar
2 cups/500 ml milk
3 sheets of gelatin
½ cup water
7 oz/200 g cape gooseberries
1 pomegranate
2 cups/500 ml heavy cream
one drop of almond extract (optional)

For the shortbread:
(see basic recipe)
2 cups/250 g flour

6½ tbsp/100 g sugar
½ cup/125 g butter
3 tbsp water
a pinch of salt

For the papaya sauce:
1 papaya
juice of ½ lemon
6½ tbsp/100 g sugar

For the garnish:
10 cape gooseberries
a few pomegranate seeds

Serves	*6*
Preparation time:	*45 minutes*
Cooking time:	*35 minutes*
Chilling time:	*2 hours*
Difficulty:	★ ★ ★

These appealing tarts are very refreshing. They are even better after spending the night in the refrigerator.

The cape gooseberries used in this recipe can be replaced by litchis, mango or guava. If using any of these fruit as substitutes, they should not be puréed before being added to the milk.

When draining the almonds, as much milk as possible should be extracted. This almond milk gives the tartlets their intense flavor. Because almonds alone are very flavorful, our chef recommends adding other flavorings, such as spices or liqueurs. There must be no lumps in the gelatin. One way to prevent this is to dissolve the gelatin in warm water before adding it to the blancmange mixture.

The skin and juice of pomegranates serve as the base for certain dyes in the carpet and textile industries of the Far East. The seeds will dye the other ingredients they touch, so they should be added at the last minute.

The colors of the fruits in this recipe will create a dazzling garnish for these tartlets.

1. Combine the crushed almonds with the sugar. Bring the milk to a boil and stir in the almond/sugar mixture. Let this cool and refrigerate overnight. Strain the milk through a thin wire mesh to remove the almonds, pressing out as much milk as possible. Dissolve the gelatin in a little water. Heat the almond milk for about 5 minutes and stir in the gelatin; let cool.

2. Prepare the shortbread as described in the basic recipe but substituting the ingredients listed above. Let it rest for 30 minutes. Roll out the dough and fit it into small tart pans. Bake twice for 15 minutes each time. Set aside 10 cape gooseberries and dice the rest. Remove the seeds from half a pomegranate and set those aside as well.

Tartlets

3. Whip the cream and fold it into the almond milk, adding a drop of almond extract if desired. Make the papaya sauce by blending the fruit with the lemon juice and sugar. Strain through a thin wire mesh and set aside.

4. Gently fold the cape gooseberries into the almond cream. Fold in the pomegranates at the last minute. Fill each tartlet shell and decorate with sliced cape gooseberries and pomegranate seeds. Refrigerate for 2 hours. Serve with the papaya sauce.

Mandarin Orange

4 mandarin oranges

For the sweet short pastry:
(see basic recipe)
1¾ cups/200 g flour
6½ tbsp/100 g sugar
6½ tbsp/100 g butter
2 eggs
a pinch of salt
zest of ½ lime
zest of ½ orange

For the sabayon filling:
2 eggs
4 egg yolks
⅓ cup/80 g sugar
6½ tbsp/100 ml rum
½ tsp/2 g saffron

For the garnish:
a few threads of saffron

Serves	*6*
Preparation time:	*40 minutes*
Resting time:	*30 minutes*
Cooking time:	*45 minutes*
Difficulty:	★ ★

Saffron is one of the most expensive spices on the market. To produce 11 pounds of fresh saffron threads, which will in turn yield 2.2 pounds/1 kilogram of dried powder, an astonishing 420,000 flowers must be harvested! Saffron has a subtle but unique flavor and is also a powerful dye.

Even today, in the small village of Mancha, the harvest of saffron is cause for celebration. Contests are held to determine the quickest and best picker. A good deal of skill is needed to harvest the flowers, for they must not be crushed when picked. They are then dried and wrapped in small packets. Some say that saffron merchants remove saffron from the market to artificially hike the price, similar to what happens with gold during economic crises.

The most difficult step of this recipe is preparing the sabayon, the egg-based filling, which needs to thicken without cooking. The sabayon can be prepared in a double boiler, which will help prevent the eggs from cooking. Adding two table-spoons of crème fraîche will make the filling creamier. To inten-sify the flavor of the mandarin ornage and to soften that of the saffron, our chef has added orange and lemon zest to the filling.

Broiling the tarts at the end will add a little color. These tarts are best served warm.

1. Prepare the sweet short pastry as described in the basic recipe but substituting the ingredients listed above, including the lime and orange zest. Let the dough rest for 30 minutes, then roll it out and prick it with a fork. Fit it into tart forms and bake it twice, for 10 minutes each time, at 390 °F/200 °C. In a bowl, beat the egg yolks and sugar until frothy, then stir in the rum.

2. Whisk the egg mixture briskly over low heat for 10 minutes, re-moving the pan from time to time to prevent the eggs from cooking. Stir in the saffron.

Tartlets with Saffron

3. Peel the mandarin oranges and separate them into sections. Place the sections in the tart shells.

4. Spoon the sabayon filling over the fruit sections. Bake for 15 minutes at 355 °F/180° C. Sprinkle each tartlet with a few threads of saffron when removing them from the oven and serve warm.

Mango

⅓ cup/80 g butter
⅓ cup/80 g sugar
2 eggs
½ cup/80 g finely ground almonds
⅔ cup/80 g flour
3½ tbsp/50 ml passion fruit liqueur
2 large mangoes

Serves   4
Preparation time: 15 minutes
Cooking time: 20 minutes
Difficulty: ★

Mangoes most likely originated in the foothills of the Himalayas. Mango is considered the national fruit of India, and has been grown there for more than 4,000 years. The Portuguese brought mangoes to Brazil in the 1700s during the era of colonization and world trade. Mangoes are usually picked when their skin is a deep yellow and their flesh is ripe, but they can be picked when they are still hard and allowed to ripen at room temperature. Like apples and lemons, mangoes are rich in vitamins A and C.

Guava or persimmons can be used in this recipe instead of mangoes, though they should not be too ripe or they will lose their original shape when baked. Rum can replace the passion fruit liqueur, which will give the almond-based dough a very distinctive flavor. Shortbread, short pastry or puff pastry can all be used here, though the combination of mango and almonds in these tarts led our chef to devise his own dough. If the tart pans are buttered and floured, the tarts will be sure to come out very easily. A small amount of melted butter should be brushed in the pans and flour sprinkled over the butter.

This sophisticated dessert, accompanied by tea or coffee, will invigorate your guests for the evening's entertainment!

1. Soften the butter. Add the sugar, eggs, almonds, flour and liqueur to the softened butter. Stir until the mixture is smooth.

2. Peel the mangoes and remove the pits. Cut into thin slices.

Tarts

3. Butter and flour each tart pan, and spoon in the almond batter.

4. Arrange the mango slices in a circular shape on the batter. Bake at 390 °F/200 °C for 20 minutes. Serve warm.

Upside-Down

1 pineapple
6½ tbsp/100 g brown sugar
2 tbsp butter
⅓ cup/60 g raisins
1 tsp nutmeg
a pinch of cinnamon
6½ tbsp/100 ml light rum
1 egg

For the sweet short pastry:
(see basic recipe)
2 cups/250 g flour
½ cup/125 g butter
½ cup/125 g sugar
1 tbsp vanilla sugar
a pinch of salt

Serves	*6*
Preparation time:	*35 minutes*
Resting time:	*20 minutes*
Cooking time:	*40 minutes*
Difficulty:	*★*

In this recipe, the raisins are soaked in a sweet syrup which lends them a delicate flavor. Our chef recommends raisins inported from Greece, which are small, dark and seedless. In some European countries, they are used to make wine. The raisins used in this recipe can also be replaced with diced dates.

One way to tell if a pineapple is ripe is to pull on the leaves. If they are easy to remove, the pineapple is ripe. After peeling the pineapple, the little black dots should be removed as well as the core of the pineapple, to produce a smooth homogeneous filling. Sautéing the diced pineapple will allow any excess juice to evaporate, which will prevent the crust from becoming soggy while it bakes.

The pie should be ummolded while it is still hot, and then returned to the oven for a few minutes until it turns golden brown. A delightful variation is to cut a small hole on the top of the pie and pour some vanilla cream or custard into it.

This dessert is delicious served warm, with vanilla or rum raisin ice cream on the side.

1. Prepare a sweet short pastry as described in the basic recipe but using the ingredients listed above. Let it rest 20 minutes, then roll out the pastry and fit it into a buttered cake pan, leaving some hanging over the edge. Cut a circle out of the remaining pastry with the same diameter as the pan for the top. Peel and dice the pineapple and sprinkle with brown sugar.

2. Sauté the pineapple in the butter until golden brown.

Pineapple and Raisin Pie

3. Stir in the raisins and spices and continue to sauté (total cooking time should be around 10 minutes).

4. Stir in the rum with a wooden spoon and then flambé it. Drain the fruit and place it in the crust. Seal the pie with the circle of pastry, brushing beaten egg between the edges of the 2 crusts and pinching them together. Bake at 355 °F/180 °C for 30 minutes.

Orange and

For the short pastry:
(see basic recipe)
1⅔ cups/200 g flour
6½ tbsp/100 g butter
1 egg
2 tbsp water
1 vanilla bean
8 tsp/40 g sugar
a pinch of salt

For the puff pastry:
(see basic recipe)
1¼ cups/150 g flour
5 tbsp/75 ml water
a pinch of salt
7½ tbsp/110 g butter

Serves	4
Preparation time:	40 minutes
Resting time:	30 minutes
Cooking time:	2 hours 50 minutes
Difficulty:	★ ★

For the filling:
2 lb 8 oz/1.2 kg oranges
3½ tbsp/50 g butter
5 tbsp/70 g sugar
1 tbsp cumin
1 egg

For the garnish:
6½ tbsp/100 ml water
3½ tbsp/50 g sugar
1 slice of orange

Cumin is often mistaken for caraway, but they are two very different spices. Cumin is stronger, warmer and slightly more bitter. It is sold in seeds or powdered form, and is most often used with grilled fish and meats. Cumin is also excellent in certain breads and cheeses, or with onions or tomatoes. In this cake, whether seeds or powder are used, our chef suggests adding the cumin near the end of the cooking so that it retains its flavor. The combination of cumin and oranges is particularly successful, as it is with most other citrus fruits. Many different varieties of oranges can be used. The sweet navel orange and blood orange are available as early as November. Other oranges are available throughout the winter, though some do not reach their peak until April. Bitter oranges should be avoided and used only in marmalades. Grapefruit or another citrus fruit can also be used, though the quantity of sugar should be changed accordingly.

This dessert can be eaten warm or cold. If served cold, a few sheets of gelatin should be added during preparation, which will make a more attractive presentation.

1. Prepare the short pastry as described in the basic recipe but substituting the ingredients listed above. Let it rest for 30 minutes. Prepare the puff pastry, also using the ingredients listed above. Dice the unpeeled oranges. Save 1 slice for the garnish and candy it in the water and sugar (see basic recipe for sugar syrup).

2. In a large pot, combine the diced oranges, butter and sugar. Gently cook them, without letting the oranges caramelize, for about 1½ hours. About 15 minutes before they are done, stir in the cumin.

Cumin Pie

3. Roll out the short pastry and prick it with a fork. Fit it into a buttered high-sided pan. Fill the crust with the sautéed oranges and fold the edge of the dough back over the oranges. Brush a little water or beaten egg around the folded edge.

4. Cut out a circle of puff pastry large enough to cover the oranges. Press it firmly on the edges of the short pastry so they adhere to one another. Decorate with a knife point and brush a beaten egg on the top, if desired. Make a small hole in the center to allow steam to escape. Bake for 10 minutes at 390 °F/200 °C, then 50 minutes at 355 °F/180 °C.

Passion

1 lb/500 g passion fruit
1 egg

For the lightly leavened dough:
(see basic recipe)
1⅔ cups/200 g flour
6½ tbsp/50 g cornstarch
2 tsp baking powder
½ cup plus 2 tbsp/150 g sugar
13 tbsp/200 g butter
2 eggs
½ cup dark rum
juice of ½ lemon

For the cream:
6½ tbsp/50 g cornstarch
3 egg yolks
6½ tbsp/100 g sugar
2 cups/500 ml milk

Serves	8
Preparation time:	35 minutes
Cooking time:	45 minutes
Chilling time:	30 minutes
Difficulty:	★ ★

The passion fruit is said to have been given its unusual name because its harvest coincides with time of the year of The Passion in the bible. When ripe, its skin is purple. Passion fruit keeps for ten to fifteen days in the refrigerator and is good to eat as long as the skin has no mold on it. It is most often used to make juice or sorbet.

Adding cinnamon, nutmeg or even ginger will intensify the flavor of the cream and certainly enchant any guest. Guava, mango or papaya can replace passion fruit for an exciting modification of this recipe. The key to successful dough lies in its perfect homogeneity. To accomplish this, the butter should be softened a few seconds in the microwave or near a source of heat. This will help it combine with the other ingredients. If the dough sticks to the edge of the bowl, add a little flour. Once mixed, the dough should be allowed to rise at room temperature. The time suggested by our chef is only an estimation, and the actual time will vary according to the particular conditions of the kitchen.

Cornstarch gives body to the cream. It must be thoroughly mixed into the cream to prevent it from gathering at the bottom of the pan, which will impair the taste of the cream and dominate the flavor of the fruit.

1. To make the dough, combine the flour, cornstarch, baking powder and sugar. Slice the butter. Add the butter, one egg at a time, the rum and the lemon juice. Stir the dough until it no longer sticks to the sides of the bowl. Form 2 balls and let rest for 1 hour.

2. To make the cream, combine the cornstarch, egg yolks and sugar. Pour the milk into a saucepan and stir in the egg yolk mixture bit by bit. Slowly bring the milk to a boil while stirring constantly and remove from heat a few seconds after it begins to boil. Let it cool for 30 minutes. Halve the passion fruit and remove all the pulp.

Fruit Ring

3. Make a flat circle with one of the balls of dough and lie it in the bottom of a bundt pan. Indent the dough in the center in order to make room for the cream. Pour the cream on the dough, and brush a beaten egg yolk along the edge. Make another flat circle of the same size with the other ball.

4. Spread the passion fruit on the cream. Cover with the second ring of dough and seal them together around the edge. Bake for 5 minutes at 430 °F/220 °C and then at 355 °F/180 °C for 35 minutes. Cool completely before unmolding.

Caribbean

For the puff pastry:
(see basic recipe)
1⅔ cups/200 g flour
6½ tbsp/100 ml water
10 tbsp/150 g butter
a pinch of salt

For the choux pastry:
(see basic recipe)
1¼ cups/150 g flour
½ cup/125 g butter
1 cup/250 ml water
2 tbsp sugar
4 large eggs
a pinch of salt

For the filling:
½ cup/70 g raisins
3½ tbsp/50 ml dark rum
5¼ oz/150 g pineapple, diced

For the pastry cream:
(see basic recipe)
¾ cup/200 ml milk
1 vanilla bean
3½ tbsp/50 g sugar
4 tsp/10 g flour
2 tsp/5 g cornstarch
2 egg yolks

Serves	8
Preparation time:	35 minutes
Cooking time:	45 minutes
Chilling time:	30 minutes
Difficulty:	★ ★

Pineapple is often used as an accompaniment to rich meats in traditional Caribbean cooking. When served as a dessert, it is best to slice it lengthwise in order to distribute the sweet and tart portions evenly. Pineapple is a healthy fruit, rich in vitamin A & B and is a tasty and popular snack. It does not tolerate cold temperatures, however, and it is best to avoid refrigerating it.

Adding the pastry cream to the choux pastry gives it a lighter consistency and helps it stay moist when baked. The baking is done in two steps, at two different temperatures. When the pie has developed a good color, the oven temperature can be lowered to allow the filling to cook. Our chef recommends cutting the vanilla bean in half before seeping it in the milk to give more flavor to the pastry cream. Also, he warns that care must be taken when adding flour to the dough to prevent it from sticking to the work surface and hands. If too much flour is added this will affect the consistency of the dough.

The edges of the pie should be trimmed to remove excess dough and to avoid large, uneven chunks. The top and edges of the pie should be brushed with egg yolk, which will also strengthen the pie as a whole. When decorating this dessert, a drop of coffee can be added to the beaten yolk to accent some areas of the crust, such as the decorative palm tree. The garnish is entirely up to the chef's imagination.

1. Prepare the choux pastry as described in the basic recipe but substituting the ingredients listed above. Because it is difficult to make small amounts of choux pastry, there will be enough to use in another dessert. Make the puff pastry as described in the basic recipe, again using the ingredients listed above.

2. Prepare the pastry cream as described in the basic recipe but using the ingredients listed above. Combine the choux pastry and pastry cream. Soak the raisins in rum for 30 minutes.

Pie

3. Stir the diced pineapple and raisins into the pastry cream. Roll out the puff pastry and fit ⅔ of it into a buttered pan, letting some hang over the edges. Pour the filling into the crust and fold the edges over the filling. Brush the edges with a beaten egg. Make a square with most of the remaining dough and close the pie, pressing firmly to seal the top and bottom together.

4. With the extra pastry, cut out a palm tree. Brush with beaten yolk. Brush the top of the pie with beaten yolk and gently press the palm tree onto it. Bake for 5 minutes at 430 °F/220 °C and then for 1 hour at 355 °F/180 °C. Refrigerate for 2 hours before serving.

For the crêpe batter:
(see basic recipe)
1 cup/125 g flour
1 cup/250 ml beer
2 eggs
a pinch of salt
⅓ cup/80 g sugar
1 orange
4 tsp butter

For the shortbread:
(see basic recipe)
1⅔ cups/200 g flour
6½ tbsp/100 g butter
a pinch of salt
3–4 tbsp water

For the filling:
2 oranges
1 lime
1 grapefruit

For the sabayon:
3 egg yolks
5 tbsp/70 g sugar
¾ cup/200 ml orange juice
zest of ½ lime

Serves   6
Preparation time: 2 hours
Cooking time: 25 minutes
Chilling time: 1 hour 30 minutes
Difficulty: ★ ★

The use of three different citrus fruits in this recipe leaves plenty of room to play with their varying levels of tartness and similar yet distinct flavors. The amount of sugar used should be changed to accommodate the particular fruits used.

An 8 in/20 cm pan with a high edge should be used to assemble this dessert. What makes this pie unique is the combination of two very different pastries, each with a distinctive texture: the crunchiness of the shortbread and the tenderness of the crêpes. Using milk instead of beer in the crêpe batter will make it even more moist.

The only tricky part of this recipe is the cream filling, or sabayon. It should be made at the last minute, just before baking the pie. The sabayon must be completely cooked before the pie is removed from the oven.

The garnish should always be made of the same fruits used in the filling, in proportion to the amount of each contained in the filling. Citrus fruit sections and slices of thin julienned zest arranged on the pie are very attractive. A sharp paring knife is ideal for cutting thin, precise strips of zest from the citrus fruits. It will also be helpful when making the julienne.

1. Prepare the crêpe batter by combining all the ingredients except the butter. Melt the butter and stir it into the batter, then let it rest for 30 minutes. Make the shortbread as described in the basic recipe but substituting the ingredients listed above. Also let rest for 30 minutes. Roll out the dough and fit it into a pan. Bake it twice, for 10 minutes each time, at 390 °F/200 °C.

2. Fill the crust with half of the crêpe batter and bake it for 5 minutes at 390 °F/200 °C. Peel the fruit and remove all the membranes. Cut out each section and reserve a few for the garnish.

Crêpe Pie

3. To make the sabayon, blanch the egg yolks with the sugar in a double boiler. Stir in the orange juice and the grated lime zest. Whisk the mixture until it thickens. Pour the remaining crêpe batter into a separate pan and cook over high heat to make a thick crêpe.

4. Arrange the citrus sections in the crust. Spoon the sabayon over them and seal the pie with the crêpe. Decorate the top with the reserved sections and zest. Refrigerate for 1½ hours before serving.

Orange and

14 oz/400 g pumpkin
1⅓ cups/150 g pecans
1 orange
½ cup/120 g butter
3 eggs
¾ cup plus 1 tbsp/200 g sugar
1 cup/120 g flour
1½ tsp baking powder
¾ cup/80 g finely ground almonds

For the short pastry:
(see basic recipe)
2 cups/250 g flour
6½ tbsp/100 g butter
1 egg
2 tbsp water
a pinch of salt

Serves	*6*
Preparation time:	*30 minutes*
Cooking time:	*1 hour*
Difficulty:	★

Pumpkin is a versatile vegetable which shows up in both sweet and savory dishes, and is an integral part of African and Caribbean cooking. Low in calories, pumpkin can be eaten raw or cooked, but is most often found in baked dishes.

Unripe pumpkin can be made into jam. Pumpkin leaves are similar to sorrel. The flesh can be removed from a pumpkin shell to create a dramatic serving bowl.

Pecans, which are similar to walnuts in many ways, are mainly grown in the United States. Our chef has chosen the pecan for this recipe because its flavor is more subtle than that of the walnut.

The combination of pecans and almonds will mask the sharpness of the orange and liven up the occasionally bland flavor of the pumpkin.

For the final garnish, this bread can be adorned with pumpkin "petals" which are made simply by cutting out shapes from the pumpkin with a cookie cutter. They should be candied for about ten minutes in sugar syrup (see basic recipe). Once drained, you can arrange them around the bread and augment them with other candied fruit. This pumpkin bread can be served either on a platform of short pastry or simply on a long serving dish accompanied with a few slices of kiwi.

1. Peel, seed and cube the pumpkin. Coarsely chop the pecans. Remove the zest of 1 orange and slice it into julienne. Reserve about 1 tbsp of the zest. Squeeze the orange and save the juice.

2. Let the pumpkin, butter and orange juice simmer together for about 20 minutes. Purée the cooked pumpkin. Make the short pastry as described in the basic recipe but substituting the ingredients listed above and let it rest for 30 minutes. Roll out the pastry and cut out decorative shapes. Bake them for 15 minutes at 355 °F/180 °C.

Pumpkin Nut Bread

3. Separate the eggs and beat the egg yolks with the sugar until the mixture doubles in volume. Stir in the pumpkin purée. In a separate bowl, combine the flour, baking powder, almonds, orange zest and chopped pecans. Stir this into the pumpkin purée.

4. Beat the egg whites until firm. Fold them into the pumpkin batter. Pour this mixture into a non-stick pan and bake for 25 minutes at 355 °F/180 °C. Once cooled, unmold and place the bread on the pastry. Garnish with raw pumpkin and kiwi and serve warm.

Mamey Bread

3 mameys
4 tbsp honey
1 tbsp water
1 licorice stick
1⅔ cups/400 ml milk
3 eggs
3 egg yolks
3½ tbsp/50 g sugar
2½ cups/600 ml cream
12 slices of white bread
2 tsp/10 g butter

Sponge cake: (see basic recipe)

For the garnish:
a few pinches of brown sugar

Serves	*6*
Preparation time:	*45 minutes*
Cooking time:	*1 hour 20 minutes*
Difficulty:	*★*

Crystallized sugar, straight from sugar cane, comes in the form of a flaky loaf. It has a dark color and a slightly rum-like taste from the residue. This dark sugar, when braised with a hot iron, will impart an excellent flavor. If an iron is unavailable, one can heat the bottom of a heavy, preferably cast-iron, pan and place it on the sugar to caramelize it.

A prized fruit of the Caribbean, mamey is the size of a small melon. It is often used to make jams, sorbets and juice. In this recipe, the thick skin should be removed. If mamey is not available, apricots can be substituted. This recipe is an excellent use for stale white bread, which works as well as fresh.

The sponge cake should be made a day in advance, or to save time, store-bought cake or even additional white bread may be used in its place.

The aroma of the licorice increases as it bakes and the sweet scent of the licorice/mamey combination will spread throughout the house to linger while the pudding is eaten.

1. Peel, pit and dice the mameys. Sauté them gently for about 10 minutes with the honey and water. Set them aside and deglaze the pan with water to make a sauce.

2. Let the licorice soak in the warm milk for about 10 minutes. Beat the eggs, egg yolks, sugar, cooled milk and cream together. Soak the bread slices in this mixture.

Pudding

3. Butter a high-sided baking pan. Slice 2 pieces of sponge cake, one the size of the bottom of the pan and the other slightly larger for the top. Place the smaller one in the pan and arrange the soaked bread slices around the edges.

4. Spoon the sautéed mamey on the bottom of the sponge cake and cover with the extra pieces of soaked bread. Pour in the remaining flavored milk. Cover with the larger piece of sponge cake and bake for 1 hour at 355 °F/180 °C. Sprinkle the surface with brown sugar when removing the pudding from the oven and caramelize with an iron.

Guava

For the puff pastry:
(see basic recipe)
1⅔ cups/200 g flour
6½ tbsp/100 ml water
10 tbsp/150 g butter
a pinch of salt

For the filling:
7 oz/200 g guava
8 tsp/40 g brown sugar
1 tsp *poudre de colombo*

For the almond cream:
¼ cup/60 g butter
½ cup plus 2 tbsp/60 g finely ground
  almonds
¼ cup/60 g sugar
1 egg
1 vanilla bean

For the garnish:
2 tbsp/20 g green pistachios
2 egg yolks

Serves	*6*
Preparation time:	*30 minutes*
Cooking time:	*35 minutes*
Difficulty:	★

Vol-au-vent is a classic puff pastry creation, originally filled with savory meat and sauce combinations. Making puff pastry is a true art, which requires strictly following each step of the process. You should make a total of six "turns" in which the dough is combined with the fat (butter or shortening) and then allowed to rest. The directions in the basic recipe should be carefully followed so that each turn is executed properly.

Guava contains high levels of vitamins A & B as well as phosphorus. Guava is used to make many refreshing juice drinks and sorbets. For this recipe, try to use firm, yellow guavas. Their slightly tart flavor will be accentuated by the

poudre de colombo, a mixture of spices common in the French Caribbean islands. The *vol-au-vent* can be decorated with the tip of a knife. The pastry should rise uniformly as it bakes. To guarantee this, ramekins can be placed in the center of the dough so that the center does not rise. Any excess vanilla can easily be used to flavor milk in another recipe.

The sliced guavas should be carefully arranged in the crust, and the space in the center should be filled with a slice of guava of the appropriate size. The coarsely ground pistachios should be scattered in a crown shape, or any other shape desired.

1. Prepare the puff pastry. Roll out half of it and cut out a 10 in/25 cm circle. Brush the edges with an egg yolk. Roll out a second circle of the same size and cut out a ring from that, about 1 in/2.5 cm wide, to place on the original circle. Brush the underside of the ring with egg yolk before laying it on the original circle.

2. On a slightly moist cookie sheet, bake the vol-au-vent for 5 minutes at 430 °F/220 °C, then for 15 minutes at 340 °F/170 °C. Soften the butter for the almond cream. In a large bowl, briskly combine the butter, finely ground almonds and sugar. Stir in the egg and vanilla.

Vol-Au-Vent

3. Fill the cooled vol-au-vent with a layer of almond cream.

4. Peel and slice the guavas and arrange them on the almond cream. Bake for 15 minutes at 340 °F/170 °C. Sprinkle the surface with brown sugar and poudre de colombo. If the guavas do not develop a thin caramel coating, broil them briefly. Garnish with the pistachios.

Glossary

ALMOND FLOUR: Blanched almonds which have been ground to a powder. Almond flour is sold commercially or can be made by chopping blanched almonds in a food processor until they have a powdery consistancy.

APRICOT GLAZE: Hot, strained apricot jam can be spread onto pastries, either as a glaze or as an isolating layer between cake and moist cream or fruit fillings.

BAIN-MARIE: Also called water bath, a gentle method of heating used to either cook food or keep food warm, a bain-marie consists of a pan containing food placed inside a larger pan of warm (not boiling) water, surrounding the smaller pan with heat. Placed in an oven, a bain-marie generates steam for foods that require moister heat than that generated by home ovens.

BISCUIT: The French word for sponge cake.

TO BLANCH: Briefly immersing foods in boiling water and then immediately in cold water to stop the cooking. This process makes it easier to remove peels and skins, rids food of impurities, and preserves the flavor and color of food before freezing.

BLINI PAN: A small cast iron pan approximately 5 in/13 cm in diameter with a thick bottom and high sides which is used to make blinis. Blini pans are also used to caramelize the tops of custards by heating the pan and placing it directly on a sugared surface.

BLINIS OR BLINTZES: Small savory pancakes made with white and buckwheat flour and leavened with yeast.

BRICK PASTRY: see *Feuille de brick*.

BRIOCHE: A classic French yeast bread, very light, yet made rich by eggs and butter.

CARAMEL: Caramel is produced when sugar is heated to 320-350 °F/160-177 °C and becomes light to dark brown. Other ingredients like water, cream and butter are added to the caramel to make sauces or candies, but liquid must be added carefully and gradually to sugar heated to these temperatures!

TO CARAMELIZE: To heat sugar until it becomes caramel (see above); or to coat something with caramel syrup; or to sprinkle sugar on the surface of a dessert and then broil or grill it briefly until the sugar turns into caramel (for example, a crème brûlée).

CHANTILLY: A term from French culinary vocabulary, *à la chantilly* means that a dish, sweet or savory, is served with or incorporates whipped cream. Crème chantilly is simply whipped cream, most often lightly sweetened with vanilla, sugar or liqueurs.

CHOUX PASTRY: A simple but unique dough that is prepared on the stovetop by bringing water or milk to a boil, adding flour and then beating in several eggs to form a sticky paste. This is the classic cream puff pastry.

CLARIFIED BUTTER: Butter that has been melted slowly without stirring, then skimmed and decanted, leaving the milk solids and water in the pan. This liquid is pure butter fat and has a higher smoking point than whole butter, but less intense buttery flavor.

TO CLARIFY: To remove any particles which interfere with the clear appearance of liquids (i.e. jelly or consommé), usually by straining or binding the impurities, often by adding and then straining out egg white.

TO COAT: In baking, coating refers to covering the surface of cakes and pastries with a thin layer often of chocolate or marzipan.

CONFECTIONERS' SUGAR: American term for icing sugar, also known as powdered sugar.

COULIS: A thick sauce consisting primarily of puréed fruit, occasionally with lemon juice, sugar or other ingredients added to enhance its flavor.

CRÈME FRAÎCHE: A thickened cream with an incomparably smooth texture and nutty, not sour, taste. If not readily available, crème fraîche can be simulated by adding 1 tsp–1 tbsp buttermilk to 1 cup heavy cream and letting the mixture stand at room temperature 8–24 hours until thickened. This will keep up to 10 days in the refrigerator.

TO DEGLAZE: To use a liquid such as water, fruit juice, alcohol or stock to dissolve food particles remaining in a pan after food has been sautéed in it. This liquid is normally used as the basis of a sauce.

TO DICE: To cut fruit or vegetables into even, dice-like shapes. Traditionally, dice is about ¼–½ in/5 mm in size.

DOUBLE BOILER: A double boiler consists of two pans that nestle into each other. The bottom pan is filled with simmering water and the top pan rests over, but not in, the hot water, providing the gentle heat necessary to melt or cook delicate foods like custards or sauces. Compare to bain-marie.

FEUILLE DE BRICK: A paper-thin crêpe made with boiled semolina flour. Feuille de brick are made by spreading a thin layer of semolina dough onto a hot griddle and removing it almost immediately, before it browns. Feuille de brick are used for crispy outer casings of desserts in place of phyllo dough or puff pastry.

FEUILLETÉ: A French word meaning "flaky" and often used to refer to pastries which are made with rich, many-layered puff pastry. See also *Millefeuille*.

TO FLAMBÉ: To pour alcohol over food and light the alcohol, imparting a very special flavor. This can be a dramatic presentation or an earlier step in the cooking process.

TO FLOUR: Also called dusting, this means coating a greased baking pan with a very fine layer of flour so that the item baked in it can be more easily removed. Other ingredients can be used instead of flour including, for example, sugar, bread crumbs, sesame seeds, or finely ground almonds.

TO FOLD: Also to blend; a means of combining two mixtures of varying densities (for example, egg whites and custard). With the lighter mass on top of the heavier one, use a spatula to cut through both, scrape along the bottom of the bowl, and up the side. Continue this, rotating the bowl slightly with each stroke. Folding must be done carefully, gently, and yet rapidly to retain the volume of the lighter mixture.

FRANGIPANE: A variation of pastry cream that is usually flavored with ground almonds and used in various cakes and pastries.

FROMAGE BLANC: A mild fresh cheese similar to cottage cheese in flavor, but not in texture. Fromage blanc has a silky, smooth texture like that of sour cream.

GANACHE: An extraordinary, rich chocolate cream made by heating whipping cream and allowing chocolate to melt in it. Depending on its texture, ganache can be used as a coating, filling, or sauce.

TO GARNISH: Decorating a dish to make it more visually appealing with various edible elements; also refers to the decoration itself. Garnish varies from a single sprig of mint, to the additions to a soup, to entire side dishes.

GELATIN: A clear and flavorless substance used to jell liquid mixtures. Gelatin is available in ¼ oz/7 g envelopes of granules (more common in North America) and in paper-thin sheets or leaves (standard in Europe). Leaf gelatin should be soaked in cold water for 5–10 minutes, then thoroughly wrung out before, like ground gelatin, being dissolved in a small amount of hot liquid before use. One envelope of granules or 4 leaves of gelatin is generally sufficient to jell 2 cups/500 ml liquid.

GÉNOISE: A variation of sponge cake, in which whole eggs are beaten with sugar to the ribbon stage (see ribbon stage) before flour, finely-ground nuts, or other ingredients are folded in.

GLACÉ: A French term meaning chilled, iced or frozen.

To GLAZE: To spread a thin layer of eggs, jelly or jam, gum arabic, or any other kind of coating onto foods to give them a shiny finish.

To GREASE OR BUTTER: Brushing a thin layer of butter or some other fat onto baking pans so that the finished product can be removed from the pans without tearing.

HEAVY CREAM: This is the American term for double cream.

HOT OVEN: 400–425 °F or 205–220 °C

To INFUSE: see to steep

INSTANT CUSTARD MIX: Unsweetened instant custard mix, also called "*poudre à flan*." Bird's English Custard Mix is one brand available on the market.

ITALIAN MERINGUE: A variation of meringue made by pouring hot sugar syrup over whipped egg whites while beating continuously until the mixture has cooled completely.

To KNEAD: To thoroughly combine and work the components of a dough either by hand or with the dough hook of an electric mixer to produce a homogenous dough. It can take 15 minutes or longer to produce a smooth, elastic dough when kneading by hand.

LIGHT CREAM: This is the American term for single cream.

To LINE: To cover the inside of a mold or pan with whatever ingredient is called for. For a charlotte, ladyfingers would be used. For aspic, the mold would be lined with gelatin.

LOW OVEN: 300–325 °F or 150–165 °C

To MACERATE/MARINATE: To soak foods in an aromatic liquid (marinade) for a period of time to allow the food to take on the flavor of the liquid and become more tender. Fruits soaked in liqueur are macerated; meat or fish in a savory liquid is marinated.

MELON BALLER: A special spoon shaped like a tiny bowl used to carve circles from melons and other fruits and vegetables.

MERINGUE: A light mass of stiffly beaten egg whites, often sweetened with sugar, which can be used as an icing or topping, an element of a mousse, cream or soufflé, or baked as cookies or bases for gâteaux. See also Italian meringue.

MILLEFEUILLE: The French word literally means "thousand leaves" and refers to the multitude of buttery-light layers in perfect puff pastry. Mille-feuille is also a 3-tiered sweet consisting of puff pastry filled with cream, custard or fruit and dusted with confectioners' sugar or glazed on top. The classic version, with pastry cream, is known as a Napoleon in North America, or vanilla slice in Britain.

MODERATE OVEN: 350–375 °F or 175–190 °C

PÂTE: The French word for many kinds of mixtures in baking, including dough, batter and pastry. Short pastry is *pâte brisée*, short sweet pastry is *pâte sucrée*, crêpe batter is *pâte à crêpe*, and so forth.

To POACH: A method of cooking food by immersing it in hot, but not boiling, water or other liquid.

To PREBAKE: To bake a pie crust or pastry shell without a filling. Prick the pastry with fork and weight it down with dried beans or baking beans so it does not rise or contort while baking.

To PURÉE: To blend or mash food until it has a perfectly smooth consistency, often by means of a blender or food processor. Purée also refers to the puréed food itself.

QUENELLE: An oval-shaped scoop of mousse, ice cream or any other unctuous ingredient shaped using two soup spoons.

To RECONSTITUTE: To add liquid to dried or dehydrated foods, such as powdered milk or dried fruits and vegetables.

To REFRESH: A means of preventing foods from continuing to cook in their own heat either by immersing the cooking pan in cold water or running cold water directly onto the food immediately after removing it from the heat.

RIBBON STAGE: When beating sugar with eggs, they should reach the ribbon stage, so called because the mixture falls in silky ribbons from the whisk or beaters.

SABAYON: Also known by its Italian name, zabaglione, it is an extremely light, frothy custard consisting of egg yolks, sugar and wine or other spirits that are vigorously whisked over a gentle source of heat.

To SAUTÉ: A method of cooking in a very small amount of hot oil or other fat, usually in an uncovered pan. Food may be lightly sautéed just to brown its surface, or cooked all the way through.

SPONGE CAKE: A classic sponge cake consists of egg whites and egg yolks, each beaten separately with sugar until light and foamy, then folded together and enriched with a little flour, ground nuts, or other ingredients. There are virtually infinite variations of sponge cakes, and they form the basis of a vast array of gâteaux and other desserts.

SPUN SUGAR: Thin filaments of cooked or caramelized sugar which are "spun" by drawing them across a flat, clean surface. Spun sugar can be gathered up to make nests, garlands or other decorations for desserts.

To STEEP OR INFUSE: To soak an ingredient in a liquid, usually hot, for several minutes in order to impart its flavor to the liquid (for example, tea in hot water, or a vanilla bean in milk when making custard).

To STRAIN: To pour or press ingredients through a sieve or a piece of cheesecloth in order to remove impurities, lumps, or seeds.

SUGAR SYRUP: A solution of sugar and water that have been boiled together. It is indispensable in baking and confection-making. The density of sugar syrup varies according to the proportions of sugar and water used; unless otherwise noted the recipes in this volume call for a heavy syrup made of equal parts sugar and water.

To TEMPER: A method of preparing chocolate to be used for decorative work or coating by slowly melting it, then allowing it to partially cool, then reheating it very briefly. This complex process serves to prevent the cocoa butter contained in the chocolate from crystallizing, which would severely detract from the appearance of the finished product.

TUILE: Literally meaning "tile" in French, a tuile is a very thin wafer that is draped over an object or placed in a form while still warm and flexible, resulting in decorative cookies that can also be used as vessels for custard, mousse, etc.

VANILLA SUGAR: Sugar infused with the flavor of vanilla bean, or containing some ground vanilla. This can easily be made at home by placing one or more vanilla beans in a jar filled with sugar. After a week or two the sugar will be permeated with the aroma of vanilla.

VERY HOT OVEN: 450–475 °F or 230–245 °C

Basic Recipes

Biscuit

Ingredients:
6 eggs – 1 cup/250 g sugar – a pinch of salt – 3 tbsp warm water – 2 cups/250 g flour.

Preparation:
In a bowl, blend the eggs, sugar, salt and water until they have reached the ribbon stage. Sift the flour over the bowl and stir well. Bake at 375 °F/190 C° for 10 to 15 minutes.

Ladyfingers

Ingredients:
8 eggs, separated – 1 cup/250 g sugar – 1½ cup plus 2 tbsp/190 g flour – 1 tsp yeast

Preparation:
Beat the egg yolks with 6½ tbsp/100 g sugar. In a separate bowl, whip the egg whites with the remaining sugar until firm. Fold the beaten whites into the yolk mixture. Stir the yeast into the flour and sift over the eggs. Stir well. Bake in a ladyfinger pan or use a pastry bag to pipe onto a greased cookie sheet and bake at 350 °F/175 °C for 10-15 minutes.

Custard

Ingredients:
4 cups/1 liter milk – ¾ cup plus 1 tbsp/200 g sugar – 12 egg yolks

Preparation:
Stir half the sugar into the milk and bring to a boil. In a small double boiler, beat the egg yolks and remaining sugar. Add a few tablespoons of hot milk to the yolks, then pour them into the boiling milk. Stir continuously, without allowing the mixture to boil, until the custard coats a spoon. Remove from heat and continue stirring until completely cooled. Pour through a strainer, if desired.

Vanilla Custard

Ingredients:
3 egg yolks – 3½ tbsp/50 g sugar – 1 cup/250 ml milk – 1 vanilla bean

Preparation:
Beat the egg yolks and sugar until well-blended and free of lumps. Bring the milk to a boil. Cut the vanilla bean lengthwise and scrape out the inside. Add the bean and its flesh to the milk and let seep. Pour the milk over the egg yolks and heat to 200 °F/80 °C. Remove from heat and pour into a cool bowl to stop the cooking process.

Pastry Cream

Ingredients:
1 vanilla bean – a pinch of salt – 4 cups/1 liter milk – 6 egg yolks – ¾ cup plus 1 tbsp/200 g sugar – 1 cup/120 g flour – 3½ tbsp/25 g cornstarch

Preparation:
Slice the vanilla bean lengthwise and add it and a pinch of salt to 3 cups/750 ml of the milk. Bring to a boil for 2 minutes. In a bowl, thoroughly beat the egg yolks and sugar. Add the flour, cornstarch, and the remaining cold milk. Briskly stir the yolks while pouring in the boiling milk. Return to the pot and let boil for 3 minutes while stirring with a whisk. Let cool and refrigerate.

Whipped Cream

Ingredients:
2 cups/500 ml heavy cream – 1⅔ cups/200 g confectioners' sugar – 1 tsp vanilla extract

Preparation:
Whip the cream until it is smooth and firm, gradually adding the sugar toward the end. Stir in the vanilla extract and refrigerate until needed.

Almond Meringue

Ingredients:
5 egg whites – ¾ cup/175 g sugar – 4½ tbsp/50 g finely ground almonds – (scant 1½ cups/150 g grated coconut for Almond and Coconut Meringue)

Preparation:
Whip the egg whites with ⅓ of the sugar until firm. Beat in the finely ground almonds. Whip in the remaining sugar (and the coconut, if desired). Use a pastry bag to pipe the meringue onto wax paper. Bake at 340 °F/170 °C for 30 minutes.

Chiboust Cream

Ingredients:
pastry cream (see basic recipe) – 2 egg whites – 1 pinch of salt – 3½ tbsp/50 g sugar

Preparation:
Prepare a pastry cream. Separately, whip the egg whites with a pinch of salt to help them set. Once firm, beat in the sugar. Fold the meringue into the pastry cream.

Sponge Cake

Ingredients:
4 eggs – ½ cup/125 g sugar – 1 cup/125 g flour

Preparation:
Beat the eggs and sugar in a bowl until they are well-blended and have a pale yellow color. Place the bowl in a double boiler and beat until the mixture doubles in volume. Remove from the heat and continue to beat until completely cooled. Sift the flour over the eggs and sugar and combine well. Bake at 355 °F/180 °C for 20 minutes in an ungreased pan.

Basic Recipes

Vanilla Ice Cream

Ingredients:
4 cups/1 liter milk – ¾ cup plus 1 tbsp/200 g sugar – 10 vanilla beans – 12 egg yolks – ½ cup/125 ml crème fraîche

Preparation:
Boil the milk with half the sugar and the vanilla beans. In a separate bowl, combine the egg yolks and remaining sugar in a double boiler, then stir in a few tablespoons of boiling milk to soften its consistency. Add the rest of the milk and cook over a low flame. Beat in the crème fraîche and process in an ice cream maker.

Marzipan

Ingredients:
1¾ cups plus 2 tbsp/450 g sugar – 3½ tbsp/50 g vanilla sugar – 3⅓ cups/500 g finely chopped almonds – 4 egg whites

For the royal icing:
1 egg white – ½ cup plus 2 tbsp/150 g sugar – 1 tsp orange-flower water

Preparation:
Combine the two sugars and whisk in the almonds and egg whites. Flatten the dough to a thickness of ⅛ in/3 mm and shape or cut out a circle. For the royal icing, whip the egg white with the sugar and orange-flower water until stiff. Glaze the marzipan with the royal icing. Bake at 300 °F/150 °C for 15 minutes.

Crêpe Batter

Ingredients:
2 cups/250 g flour – 6 eggs – 2 cups/500 ml milk – 1 cup/250 ml heavy cream – 2 tbsp Grand Marnier – 1 tsp vanilla extract – ¼ cup/60 g butter

Preparation:
Form a well in the flour and break in the eggs. Combine the eggs and flour without allowing lumps to form. Add the milk, cream, Grand Marnier and vanilla extract. Slice the butter, add it to the batter and stir it in as well as possible. Let the batter rest before proceeding as directed in the recipe.

Short Butter Pastry

Ingredients:
¼ cup/30 g confectioners' sugar – 1 egg yolk – a pinch of salt – ¼ cup /60 g butter – half a vanilla bean – ¾ cup/90 g flour

Preparation:
In a food processor, combine all the ingredients except the flour until they are well-blended and have a smooth texture. Gradually add the flour and mix thoroughly. Wrap the pastry in a cloth and refrigerate it overnight, if possible, because this makes the pastry much easier to work with.

Sweet Short Pastry

Ingredients:
½ cup/125 g butter – ½ cup/125 g sugar – 2 eggs – 2 cups/250 g flour a pinch of salt

Preparation:
Soften the butter. Cream the butter, sugar and eggs. When the ingredients are well-blended, add the flour. Mix by hand until the pastry is perfectly smooth. Let sit overnight in the refrigerator. Bake twice at 390 °F/200 °C, for 10 minutes each time.

Egg-White Pastry

Ingredients:
5 tbsp/75 g butter – ¼ cup/60 g sugar – zest and juice of 1 lemon – 6½ tbsp/75 g finely ground almonds – 1¼ cups/150 g flour – a pinch of salt – 3 egg whites

Preparation:
Cream the butter and sugar. Juice the lemon and grate the zest. Add the lemon zest, almonds, flour, salt and lemon juice to the butter and sugar mixture. Separately, beat the egg whites until stiff and fold them into the pastry. Let rest 30 minutes. Proceed according to the recipe.

Puff Pastry

Ingredients:
4½ cups/550 g flour – 1 tsp salt – 1 cup/250 ml water – 1½ cups/375 g butter*

Preparation:
Make a well in the flour on a clean work surface. Pour the salt and water in the well. Mix these ingredients together without over-handling. Let the dough rest 20 minutes, then roll it out in the shape of a square on the work surface. Soften the butter and spread it on the square. Fold the 4 corners of the square over the butter. This is one "turn." Make 2 turns, refrigerating the pastry for 20 minutes in between, a total of 6 times.

* In hot climates and in tropical regions, butter should be substituted with adequate puff pastry shortening, which can be found in most grocery stores.

Short Pastry

Ingredients:
½ cup/125 g butter – 2 cups/250 g flour – 1 egg – 1 tbsp water – 6½ tbsp/50 g confectioners' sugar – a pinch of salt

Preparation:
Soften the butter, then slice it into small pieces and incorporate into the flour. Add the egg, water, sugar and salt, mixing only until blended. Excessive handling will prevent the pastry from developing an elastic consistency. Let it rest 30 minutes. Bake the dough twice, for 10 minutes each time, at 390 °F/200 °C.

Basic Recipes

Brioche

Ingredients:
1½ tbsp/10 g compressed fresh yeast* – 4 cups/500 g flour – 2 tbsp/30 g sugar – 2 tsp/10 g salt – 1½ cups plus 1 tbsp/375 g butter – 8 eggs

Preparation:
Dissolve the yeast in a little warm water, then stir in 1 cup of the flour. Keep this starter in a warm location until it doubles in volume. Combine the remaining flour with the sugar, salt, butter and 3 of the eggs. Knead the dough. Add the remaining eggs one by one. Beat by hand. Combine the egg-based dough with the yeast starter. Let sit for 4 hours. Turn the dough over and let it rest 2 additional hours. Bake at 355 °F/180 °C until it reaches the desired height and coloration.

* In hot climates and tropical regions, active dry yeast should be substituted for the compressed fresh yeast. Use half the amount called for.

Choux Pastry

Ingredients:
1 cup/250 ml milk – 1 tsp/5 g salt – 1 tsp/5g sugar – 6½ tbsp/100 g butter – 1½ cups/150 g flour – 4 large eggs

Preparation:
In a pot, bring the milk to a boil with the salt, sugar, and butter, sliced into small pieces. As soon as the butter has melted, reduce the heat to low, add the flour and stir vigorously with a wooden spoon until a homogenous liquid forms. Let it barely simmer for about 10 minutes, while stirring continuously. The pastry should pull away from the sides of the pot. When it no longer sticks to the spoon, remove from heat. Beat in the eggs, one by one, incorporating them well. The pastry should be neither too soft nor too hard. Proceed according to the recipe.

Shortbread Pastry

Ingredients:
1⅔ cups/200 g flour – a pinch of salt – ¾ cup plus 1 tbsp/100 g confectioners' sugar – 6½ tbsp/100 g butter – 5 tbsp milk or water

Preparation:
Form a well in the flour and place the salt and sugar in it. Soften and slice the butter, then add it to the flour mixture. Mix well by hand, while adding the water or milk. Knead the pastry with the palm of your hand. Form a ball and let it rest for 30 minutes. Bake twice, for 10 minutes each time, according to the recipe.

Lightly Leavened Dough

Ingredients:
1 tbsp compressed fresh yeast – ½ cup/125 ml milk – ¼ cup/60 g butter – 2 cups/250 g flour – ½ cup plus 1 tbsp/70 g confectioners' sugar – a pinch of salt – 1 tbsp orange zest

Preparation:
Stir the yeast into the lukewarm milk. Melt half the butter and add it to the milk. Add the flour and stir well. Separately, combine the remaining butter with the sugar, salt and orange zest. Combine both mixtures and knead well. Let the dough rest until it has doubled in size, then shape it as desired and bake at 355 °F/180 °C for approximately 40 minutes.

* In hot climates and tropical regions, compressed fresh yeast should be substituted by active dry yeast. Use half the amount called for.

Doughnut Batter

Ingredients:
1⅔ cups/200 g flour – 1 tsp/5 g salt – 2 eggs – 4 tsp/20 ml beer – 2½ tbsp/40 ml oil

Preparation:
Mound the flour in a large bowl and form a well in it. Add the salt, egg yolks and beer in the center. Stir the liquid with a wooden spatula, incorporating a little flour with each turn. Pour in the oil to prevent the batter from developing a crust while it is resting. Set aside in a cool place before forming the doughnuts and frying.

Sugar Syrup

Ingredients:
4 cups/1 liter water – 2½ cups/600 g sugar

Preparation:
Dissolve the sugar in the water and let it boil for 3 minutes.

Index of Recipes